A sequel to
The Chronicles of Tombstone

By

Ben T. Traywick

Published by:

Red Marie's Bookstore
P.O. Box 891
Tombstone, Arizona 85638

Designed and Printed by:

WE PRINT IT, INC.
—Los Angeles—

To the
Tombstone
Wild Bunch

Published by
Red Marie's Bookstore

Designed and Printed by
WE PRINT IT, INC.
—Los Angeles—

LEGENDARY CHARACTERS OF SOUTHEAST ARIZONA

I foretell....
that one of mine
Will come forth
to fan the flame
And that....
Chaos and Havoc
Will surely be
their name.

TABLE OF CONTENTS

Arizona Territory

1

Arizonians Were Tough

During the middle of the 1800's, men from every kind, place and walk of life drifted West. They came on horseback, by wagon, and by stagecoach.

True, they were a tough, hard-bitten breed, but then, they *had* to be to survive. Finding areas suitable to them, they began to prospect, raise cattle, or build towns.

Fierce Apaches with a lust for blood roamed the whole of the Arizona Territory. There were few military outposts and all too few soldiers to man them. In fact these soldiers were hard put to just defend their garrisons and themselves, much less any settlers foolhardy enough to venture into such a desolate, merciless land.

Savage Indians had laid claim to the valley and rugged mountains for thousands of years. It was their land and they looked upon the white men drifting in as invaders. They began to attack the isolated camps, cabins and wagon trains, killing the white men, then burning what they could not carry away.

Perhaps they would have succeeded in killing off the invaders except for the stubbornness and determination of the white men. They had moved into the valleys of Arizona and built homes and they intended to stay. To do so, they completely disregarded personal danger, were willing and even anxious to accept any risk to accomplish their objective. As a result, they faced impossible odds, performed heroic feats, and emerged victorious in encounters that appeared to offer only certain death.

One of these determined settlers was a woman.

Lewis Stevens, who owned a ranch four miles from Prescott at the Point of Rocks, had gone to attend a session of the Territorial Legislature in 1867. Mrs. Stevens was left on the ranch with only one hired hand.

About a hundred yards from the house lay a huge pile of boulders. The kitchen window, where Mrs. Stevens spent the greater part of her time, looked out upon these rocks. She often admired the way they reached toward the sky, for she loved everything about the desert country.

That afternoon, during one of her frequent glances out the window, she saw an unusual movement among the rocks. She held her eyes steadily on the spot and was soon able to distinguish an Apache warrior.

Part of her kitchen equipment, along with pots and pans, was a double-barreled shotgun. When she returned to the window, she caught sight of several more Indians gliding through the rocks. One had worked his way almost to the kitchen door. Mrs. Stevens threw open the kitchen door and gave him one barrel of buckshot. His companions, who were close behind, beat a hasty retreat to the protection of the rocks.

The blast from the shotgun brought the hired man on the run. Though the Apache Mrs. Stevens had shot was dead and some of the others were stung by buckshot, there were at least twenty Apaches in the rocks.

Like the majority of ranch houses in Arizona during those years, the Stevens' house was well built to withstand an attack and was amply stocked with guns and ammunition.

By shifting from one side of the house to the other and reloading all the guns whenever possible, Mrs. Stevens and the hired man beat off two rushes by the Apaches. Even when the savages tried to reach the corrals to run off the stock the unerring aim of the two in the house drove them back to the protection of the rocks.

The battle lasted all afternoon with the Apaches sniping from the rocks and Mrs. Stevens and the hired man returning the fire from the house. Every window in the house was shattered and all the walls pock-marked by bullets.

Late in the evening a neighbor, named Johnson, heard the firing

and rode for help. He arrived with reinforcements and routed the Apaches. Mrs. Stevens and her hired man were unhurt. She dispatched a note to her husband in Prescott that evening. It read:

"Lewis, send me some more buckshot.
I'm almost out of it."

BILLY RHODES BIG BLUFF

Billy Rhodes ran a big bluff on the Apaches and, as incredible as it seems, made it stick. Billy found some fine land down near Tubac in the Santa Cruz Valley in the 1860's. He laid claim to it and, though the Apaches wiped out Tubac during the Civil War, he vowed he'd hold on to his land come Hell or Apaches.

The renegade Apaches liked to leave the reservation and raid south into Mexico. They rode along the ridges of the Santa Catalina Mountains to Patano Wash where they descended, then began the climb to the heights of the Huachucas and the Whetstones. From their position on the ridges, they could detect any potential victims below.

A war party descended into the lowlands and raided Billy Rhodes' ranch one day. Billy was in town and his partner was alone at the ranch. He was captured by surprise before he was aware that the Apaches were about.

The Apaches were wily enough to refrain from burning the ranch. They wanted to get Rhodes, and they knew that if he saw smoke he would never ride in. So while they waited in anticipation of Billy's homecoming, they passed the time by torturing his partner.

Billy was slow in coming and by the time that the scouts warned of his approach, there was not much left of the hapless prisoner.

Day was rapidly disappearing as Billy Rhodes came down the rutted wagon road toward the house. When he was but a hundred yards away a vague finger of apprehension touched him. Though he couldn't for the life of him identify it, something was not quite right. That feeling of uneasiness persisted and Billy stopped his horse. While he was trying to consider his suspicions, a warrior, eager for the kill, threw a hasty shot at him. The bullet whizzed by Billy's head.

Before the sound of the shot had died out he had turned his horse and was racing away. Billy's pony was already tired from the long trip that day and as the Apaches swarmed to their ponies, Billy knew it would be a short race. Already he could see approximately fifty Warriors racing to intercept him. Rhodes knew that he was doomed as the only weapon he had was a pistol with six bullets.

As the Apaches drew closer, he resolved that he would take five of them with him on the glory trip. Meanwhile he was urging his jaded pony on in an attempt to reach a certain clump of willows he remembered being along the river. When he did reach it, it was as he recollected: a thick clump of trees with open ground on all sides. Throwing himself from his laboring horse, he dived head-first into the willows.

For a while the Apaches circled the thicket shouting, yelling, and brandishing their weapons. They were usually a patient, careful lot, but this time darkness was closing in on them, so they were in a hurry to get this business over. They had to rush Rhodes and finish him off within a very few minutes to beat the fall of night.

Fifty savages fell prone upon the earth and began to slither closer to the thicket where Rhodes crouched. He waited until he was sure of his target, then fired for the first time. Only forty-nine Apaches raced back to cover. Angered, the Indians rose and, uttering blood-curdling war cries, rushed the willow thicket.

Coolly, Billy raised his gun, steadied it, then pulled the trigger twice. Two Apaches hit the ground to lay motionless and the charge was broken again. For a while all was quiet, then they came again screeching and yelling as before.

Rhodes' pistol bucked twice more and the Apaches left two more dead behind when they retreated. This time, however, they had scored a hit, for Billy lay in the willows with a broken arm. One of the Apache bullets had shattered his elbow.

Taking his good arm, Billy pushed the mangled elbow as deep into the moist earth as he could and steeled himself for the next attack. Only one bullet lay between him and a terrible death by fiendish torture. The Chief of the war party led the Apaches in the next charge. Billy lined his sights on the Chief's coppery chest, followed his target a moment, then squeezed the trigger. There was a slight smile on Rhodes' face as he fired his last shell. He fully believed he had reached the end of the trail, but he did not reckon with the way the Indian mind worked, for they withdrew out of pistol range. Their Chief was already on his way to the happy hunting ground.

An internal discussion among the Apaches followed, then one called out to Billy in Spanish, "You are brave warrior. Because of this if you put down your gun and come out we will not harm you. If you do not we will come and kill you!"

Billy Rhodes, holding an empty gun and with one arm useless, ran the biggest bluff any man could.

"Damn your ornery hides," he yelled. "You come and get me! I've shot six of you and I'm plumb anxious to get me some more!"

Then he lay back waiting for the savages to overtake him. The silence continued as the shadows deepened and turned into darkness. As the time passed, Rhodes realized, in stunned amazement, that the Apaches had slipped away.

Carefully, he caught up his horse and rode into Tucson. He had won out against impossible odds and on nothing whatever but a colossal bluff.

THREE AGAINST FIFTY

Jim Price and "Whiskey" Bill were driving two wagon loads of hay to Camp Grant for Thomas Venable. Two soldiers had been sent along as an escort.

Deep in rough, rocky, canyon country, they were ambushed by a band of approximately fifty Apaches. The first fusillade of shots killed Jim Price and wounded one of the Cavalry men.

All three of the men sought protection under one of the wagons and held off a number of Apache charges with their excellent marksmanship. A second bullet tagged the already wounded soldier seriously enough to put him out of the fighting. He volunteered to try and reach help at Camp Grant. In his wounded condition, his chances of reaching his destination were not very good. Still, the chances of staying alive under the wagon weren't much to brag about either. His two companions watched him crawl away through the brush until he was lost to sight.

The remaining soldier and "Whiskey" Bill fought a raging battle with the Apaches for another three hours. Coppery, naked bodies were sprawled about the area to testify to the shooting ability of the two men. "Whiskey" Bill half-rose to get a better shot at one of the savages and a shot smashed through his chest, killing him instantly.

Left alone, the soldier knew he could not hope to hold off the Apaches so he made a run for it. He plunged into the brush with a score of Apaches on his heels.

Reaching a pile of rocks, he ducked behind them, killed the two nearest savages, then lit out again. As they gained on him he would turn and shoot the nearest Apache, then flee again.

It did not take the Apaches long to realize that this man could both run and shoot. After a few exhibitions of his abilities, they gave up the chase.

The cavalry man reached Camp Grant at sunset. Strangely enough, the wounded trooper had made it too and was in the post hospital. A hospital. A detachment, sent after the renegades, buried the two teamsters where they had fallen. James Price and "Whiskey" Bill sent along a number of their enemies to precede their path to the hereafter.

THE CIENEGA DE SOUZ INCIDENT

It was October 21, 1871 and, on the Cienega de Souz, about twenty-five miles from Fort Bowie, a story was about to unfold that can't be topped even in Arizona history.

On that date, R.M. Gilbert, a sick man who had been ill with fever for several weeks, battled sixty Apaches and managed to stay alive.

His nearest neighbor, Dick Barnes, had moved in to give him a hand during his period of illness. Though Gilbert survived the fever, he was still as weak as a kitten and confined to his bed.

Barnes had chores of his own to perform at home which was not very far away. He made Gilbert as comfortable as possible then departed, promising to return in a couple of hours. The kindly neighbor had scarcely cleared the house before Apaches, hidden in the grass and tules, ridded him with bullets.

Gilbert, suddenly endowed with an incredible strength, leaped from his bed, grabbed his Henry rifle and rushed into the yard to help his friend. The Apaches, too, were racing for Barnes' still form. The pale, skinny Gilbert charging straight at them, firing his Henry from the hip was too much for them and they retreated, probably because they thought him completely insane.

At any rate, Gilbert reached his stricken friend, effortlessly flung him over his shoulder and retreated back to the cabin, Apache bullets plucking at his clothing from every side. Carefully, he placed Barnes upon the bed and went to a window to battle the Apaches.

The Indians completely surrounded the cabin, but they could not get to the desperately fighting Gilbert. All morning he held off attack after attack with the Apaches sometimes getting close enough to poke their rifle barrels through the windows to shoot at him.

Sometime around noon, Barnes died and, soon after, a warrior sneaked close enough to shoot Gilbert in the groin. Undaunted, the sick man stuffed a piece of his shirt in the hole to stop the bleeding and crawled from window to window to shoot at the enemy.

Late in the afternoon the Apaches crept close and set fire to the building. In minutes the entire cabin was filled with flame and smoke.

Gilbert loaded his rifle and pistol and then assured himself that Barnes was dead. Then, with a weapon spitting lead in either hand he leaped out into the yard and made a dash for the tules.

He shot down two braves who blocked his path. Again he escaped in a veritable hail of bullets. He moved from place to place through the tules, managing to hold the Apaches off 'till darkness fell.

Finally, under the cover of the black night, he crawled away.

It took him all that night and the next day to crawl the fifteen miles to David Wood's hay camp. There, his wounds were tended and he lived to fight the Apaches again.

TOUGH AS STEEL

There were times when the Apaches felt a vast respect for an enemy they had killed. In such instances they did not mutilate the body.

This was the situation involving a gambler in Prescott, named Felix. People there claimed that he bought and sold rustled cattle and horses, sold whiskey and guns to the Apaches, and had, on occasion, held up a few stages. Because of these claims, no man called him friend. None had a good word for him. Yet on the day in which his life was to end, he showed that he was made of finer steel than any who thought they knew him imagined.

Felix owned a well-stocked cattle ranch, several miles out of Prescott. He had married a quiet, comely, Mexican woman who was seldom seen and the unusual couple had two children.

On the day that Felix was to show a type of courage that few men possess, he was driving his wife and children to Prescott in a buckboard pulled by a fine, spirited, team of horses.

A war party of Apaches spotted the family from the ridges and set out in pursuit.

Felix saw them long before they reached the lowlands and used the whip on his team. Unfortunately, the buckboard was restricted to the rutted road while the savages could run their ponies across the rough country at will.

It was a scant few miles to the safety of Prescott, but Felix knew that they would never make it.

When they reached a point where the road ran through a rocky canyon, he slowed the buckboard and looked fondly upon his wife and children for the last time.

"Lay the whip on 'till you reach Prescott," he instructed his wife. "I'll stop them for a while."

With those words, he leaped to the ground and ran to the rocks beside the road. He carried a Henry rifle and sixteen rounds of ammunition.

Felix's wife ran her horses to death to reach Prescott. When she told her story every man who heard it rode out in a rescue party.

When they reached the spot where the gambler made his stand, they found the bodies of fourteen Apaches sprawled in death among the rocks and brush.

Felix was dead, sixteen empty brass shells scattered around him. He had wasted only two of his shots.

The Apaches had covered his face with a piece of cloth and left him otherwise untouched, showing their admiration for Felix's bravery.

THIS HERE LAND IS MINE!

As Arizona Territory was slowly settled and civilized, other unusual incidents took place.

One such case was that of Billy Fourr who lived up near Dragoon Pass. Billy had been hauled into court for fencing off Government land.

He pleaded guilty to the charge, but insisted the land was his.

"How did you acquire this land?" the prosecutor asked.

"Took it away from the Apaches," Billy replied.

The jury, all old time Arizonians, *acquitted* him!

REFERENCE:

1. Arizona Pioneers Historical Society, files.

Albert Sieber

2

SIEBER

On the high road from the Roosevelt Dam, a mile toward Payson, stands a monument hewn from native stone by Apache laborers in memory of Al Sieber. It is near the spot where he met Death and the inscription reads:

AL SIEBER

"A Veteran of the Civil War and for twenty years a leader of scouts for the U.S. Army in Arizona Indian troubles was killed on this spot February 19th, 1907 by a falling rock during construction of the Tonto Road.

His body is buried in the cemetery at Globe."

This is but *one* memorial to the most famous scout of the Southwest. Another is erected over his grave in Globe by the Territorial Legislature.

George W.P. Hunt, who was to be the Governor of Arizona several times, introduced the bill to appropriate one hundred dollars for a monument. It weighed 2,350 pounds and is five feet six inches high.

Albert Sieber was born in Mingolsheim in the Grand Dutchy of Baden, Germany on February 29, 1844. His father died the next year and his mother, Katherina, emigrated to America with her eight children. The Sieber family settled in Lancaster, Pennsylvania. In 1856 they moved on west to Minneapolis.

When the War between the States erupted, the First Minnesota Volunteers were recruited. Sieber enlisted in Company B, First Minnesota Volunteer Infantry as soon as he was old enough on March 3, 1862. He served through the bitter fighting of the Peninsula Campaign as a sharpshooter. Sieber was described as six feet tall, weighing 180 pounds and completely devoid of fear.

Al was severely wounded in the Battle of Gettysburg on July 2, 1863. A shell fragment fractured his skull and while he was lying helpless on the battlefield, a minnie ball struck his right ankle, travelled through his leg and emerged at the knee.

His wounds were serious enough to keep him confined to the hospital until December 8, 1863. At that time, he was posted to the First Battalion, First Company, Invalid Corps, at York, Pennsylvania. In March, 1864 this Company became First Regiment, Company K, Veteran Reserve Corps, Waltham, Massachusetts.

Sieber made corporal on February 19, 1864, and was assigned provost duty. Later, he was sent to Elmira, New York to guard Rebel prisoners. Al was mustered out of the service on July 15, 1865, and was paid three hundred dollars bounty money by the State of Massachusetts.

Returning to Minneapolis, he remained there until early in 1866, at which time he started West. His first noted appearance in the West was in Virginia City, Nevada, the location of the great silver rush. Apparently, he was not successful there as he soon turned up at the new strike in White Pine, eastern Nevada. Whatever his ambitions at that time, he did not realize them in Nevada, for he moved on to California.

In the "Golden State" he joined forces with a group of adventurers, who rounded up a herd of wild horses and drove them to Arizona. After selling the horses, Sieber was out of a job again when he was offered a job as foreman of C.C. Bean's Ranch in the Williams Valley and a second Bean ranch on the Verde River.

He did well managing these ranches for awhile, but soon grew unhappy as he spent most of his time defending the ranches and livestock from renegade bandits and hostile Indians.

When a man, named Miner, formed the now famous Miner Expedition to locate some rich gold properties in 1871, Al was quick to join the endeavor. Miner claimed that he and some other men had found an area of gold deposits where seventeen ounces of gold was washed from a single shovel-full of dirt.

A party of thirty men left Prescott to go to this fabulous gold location, with Miner as their guide. Their intentions were well-known to all along their route of travel. By the time they had passed through Phoenix, Florence, and Tucson, their ranks had swelled to two hundred sixty-seven men.

They crossed the San Pedro River, moved up to the head of the San Carlos River, then over to the Salt River. Prospecting all along the way, they moved into the Tonto Basin, along Cherry Creek and up into the Sierra Ancha Mountains.

Even with all their prospecting, they found absolutely nothing. They retraced their steps back down Cherry Creek to the Salt River and over to Wheatfield then on to Pinto Creek. By this time, most of the men were disillusioned.

They had come to the conclusion Miner had no knowledge of the whereabouts of any gold and that he was just leading them on a wild goose chase.

The party of men split up and Sieber returned to Prescott in the company of men who later became famous in Arizona history. One of these men was Ed Peck, who later discovered the rich Peck Mine. Two others were the brothers Robert and Thomas Anderson, who would discover the Old Dominion Mines in Globe two years later. Governor Safford was also a member of this party.

In July, 1871, Sieber became a Scout for the U.S. Government at Camp Hualapai. While in this position, Al did some scouting for General Stoneman before he was replaced by General Crook. Captain Mason (5th Cavalry) in his field report of September 24, 1872, described the attack on four Apache-Mojave (Tonto) camps. This raid netted forty hostiles killed, several wounded, and eight women and ten children captured. Mason noted in his report that Hualapai Scouts were used in this raid, and were highly successful. He also added,

"Guide Sieber did excellent service."

Early in 1873, Sieber was transferred to Camp Verde to lead a large body of Apache Scouts in the field. By the Winter of 1873, it appeared to Sieber and his men that every hostile in Arizona was raiding somewhere. The scouts were continually moving about and fighting. Sieber would lead fifty to one-hundred Apache Scouts to attack the rampaging hostiles, he being the only white man in the force. The scouts and the hostiles met in fierce and deadly combat, neither side asking or expecting quarter.

Sieber loved the wild vastness of Arizona, and often remarked on its bountiful beauty. He said that grasses were so high along the river bottoms that a man on horseback could hide in them and that, many times in the White Mountains, he had seen huge flocks of wild turkeys, flocks that he estimated numbered ten thousand birds. When they were on a march, Al and his scouts lived off the land. In one day's march his scouts killed eighty deer, and a large number of turkey gobblers weighing up to forty pounds or more each. Only the breasts of the latter were taken and the flesh made into jerky.

While he was a scout, Al came to be an excellent judge of Indian character and to understand their complex personalities. He was quick to treat them fairly and to dispense harsh justice. He never lied to them or deceived them in any manner. He fought them when they were hostiles, then enlisted them as scouts when they came onto the reservation. In most instances, they became dependable, faithful scouts when Sieber enlisted them.

Although the business of fighting hostiles kept him extremely busy, Al was always on the alert for any evidence of mineral values. He accompanied the Tonto Apaches to the place of "bitter water' while he was Chief of Scouts under General Crook.

A tiny stream passing over limestone for countless years built up a rich deposit of copper. Sieber saw this deposit and returned at a later date with George Kell to locate a claim, calling it the Copper Queen. Years after, a large quantity of rich ore was taken from this claim.

Most likely, Sieber, George Kell, and George Hull were the first white men to follow the copper-laden stream up to the cliffs. This area was later to become the United Verde Copper Company Mine and the town of Jerome. Sieber once described his battles with the Del Shay Tontos in the Sierra Anchas. He pointed out that these Indians fought from behind rock breastworks they had constructed in various locations about Del Shay Basin. He explained that he and his Scouts would encounter a bunch of hostiles one day, kill several of them, and then next day, find the others behind another rock wall, kill some of them, then repeat the process next day. These Apaches never surrendered, but were practically exterminated.

The best tracker that Sieber ever had was a Tonto, called John Daisy. This man had the rare ability of being able to trail at night. When Daisy felt that the scouts were drawing near to a hostile camp, he would have two of his companions hold an Army blanket around him while he would strike matches to verify the trail. When he was confident that they were very near an enemy encampment, the Scouts would conceal themselves until the first light of dawn, at which time they would attack the hostiles.

At the Battle of "Cibicue" in 1881, the Apache Scouts revolted and killed Captain Hentig and several of the Troopers in his command. Although Sieber and his scouts were at Camp Verde, they were ordered to the scene of the revolt. They made forced marches, arrived in short time and recovered a pack mule heavily loaded with rifle ammunition which had been lost by the soldiers during the battle.

Sieber's Scouts aided in the capture of the guilty Apaches, three of whom were hanged at Fort Grant.

There was another outbreak from San Carlos in July, 1882. The "Broncos" went north through the Sierra Anchas to Spring Creek, killing several people who were unlucky enough to encounter them. Captain Chaffee was ordered to the scene of the trouble, Sieber and his scouts accompanying him. At Chevalon Fork, the Apaches set up an ambush for the approaching cavalrymen. However, the scouts detected the ambush before it could be sprung. Reinforced by several more troops of cavalry and eight White Mountain Scouts from Fort Apache, Chaffee plunged into battle with the hostiles.

The fight lasted all day and, when night came, rain began to fall. Under this cover, the hostiles slipped away and scattered, leaving sixteen of their number dead in the canyon.

Chief Smiley, First Sergeant of Sieber's Scouts, lost his brother in this fight. One soldier was killed and several wounded. In the fiercest part of the battle, Sieber killed three Apaches.

CHARLIE'S SQUAW

At San Carlos in the early 1880's, there was an Indian Scout named Charley, who procured a wife from another band by paying her parents her value in horses and other presents. Apparently, all involved were satisfied and Charley took his new wife to his lodge.

After only a few days of wedded bliss, the new bride returned to her people and steadfastly refused to have anything further to do with her husband. The husband, his pride destroyed and angry, demanded that the parents return the wife's purchase price. When this was refused, Charley demanded that the wife return to his lodge. When this, too, was refused, the scout was overcome with anger.

He attacked the woman and her family, injuring several of them and killing the woman. Charley was immediately arrested by the Indian Police and an Indian court was set up to judge him as was the custom at the San Carlos Agency in those days.

The Indian court dispensed swift justice, found Charley guilty and decreed that he be turned over to his wife's tribe and they would mete out the proper punishment.

As the incident had generated a great deal of bitterness between the tribes, the wife's people let it be known that Charley was to be put to death by slow torture. As the Chief of Scouts was also in charge of the guard house where Charley was confined, the hapless scout sent for Sieber.

He explained to Al that he was guilty and that he expected to die for his crime. He had no objections except that he did not wish to be tortured. Sieber was sympathetic, and promised Charley that he would not be tortured.

A large number of Indians came to the guard house to pick up their prisoner and escort him to his final end. Al asked them how they were going to put Charley to death. Their reply was that they intended to dismember him joint by joint until there were no joints left. Upon hearing this, Sieber refused to give them the prisoner. He told them that they could have Charley if they solemnly promised that they would shoot or hang him, but absolutely no torture.

The band of Indians were very angry and upset at the stand taken by Sieber, but they also knew better than to break a promise to him. They went away muttering to themselves, feeling that proper justice had been thwarted.

After awhile they sent a committee back to inform Sieber that since he had interfered and would not let them torture Charley, then he could just hang the scout for them.

Again Sieber balked, saying that he would dispose of Charley, but he had no intention of hanging him. Reluctantly, the Indians agreed.

To carry out this action, Al ordered a spring wagon. When it arrived at the guard house, he threw a pick and shovel into the back. With two of his Scouts, Smiley and Rowdy, Al put the prisoner in the wagon and set out on the road to Fort Thomas.

With the team moving briskly along, Sieber and Charley talked of past events that they had shared in these mountains. Then, as Charley looked fondly at the rocky wilderness, a shot rang out and he fell from the wagon – dead.

The three men dug a grave on the mountainside and buried him. Charley had paid his debt and, as far as Sieber was concerned the incident was closed forever.

THE SAGA OF MACHOKAY

In 1882, General Crook, Captains Chaffee and Crawford, accompanied by Al Sieber and a hundred of his Scouts, crossed into Mexico, moving toward the Sierra Madre Mountains. Sieber sent Machokay ahead with fifty scouts to try and determine the location of the hostiles. This force found the trail of two Indians and saw the hostile pony herd in the distance.

Machokay sent the information back to command, and he and a San Carlos scout, called Pasalau, moved in closer. They encountered two Chiricahua bucks with sixteen ponies. Machokay grabbed at the reins of one and told him not to run. The Apache whirled his horse and drew a pistol. Machokay shot and killed him. The other buck escaped though Pasalau shot at him.

Author's Note:

"Sergeant Pasalau later joined the band of the "Apache Kid" and lost his head as a result of that decision."

Crook's command eventually came so close that Geronimo and his band negotiated a return to the reservation. Those Apaches were found to be holding five Mexican women captive. These women were turned over to the Mexican Consul in Tucson.

Geronimo and his band went back to the reservation and were eventually relocated at Apache.

Still disgruntled, Geronimo and some of his followers broke out and started raiding again in 1885. This time, the Army pursued the hostiles into the Sierra Madres.

Captain Dorst (4th Cavalry) with Machokay and a hundred scouts and Captain Crawford with a hundred White Mountain Scouts advanced into the formidable mountains in the worst of the winter. It was extremely cold and the scouts became accustomed to icicles in their long hair.

Machokay was out on the high mountain peaks in the freezing cold, with fifteen scouts, trying to locate the hostiles, when his force was recalled because of the killing of Captain Crawford by Mexican Federal Troops.

Lieutenant Maus took command of Crawford's men and, in a week's time, they joined forces with Captain Dorst's group and both commands moved into San Carlos.

The men were gaunt, sore-footed, and their clothing tattered and shredded. Most of the scouts' enlistments were up and they were paid off and discharged. Sieber, wishing to keep the services of Machokay, offered him the position of first sergeant if he would re-enlist. The scout refused as he badly needed some rest.

Author's Note:

"Machokay eventually re-enlisted and served four more enlistments under Sieber."

THE "APACHE KID"

When Machokay refused to re-enlist, Sieber made the *"Apache Kid"* First Sergeant.

Back in the 1860's, two young Apache warriors both desired the same beautiful Apache squaw. These two warriors were called Toga-de-Chuz and Rip. The young maiden chose the former to be her husband.

Elated at this turn of events, the jubilant Toga-de-Chuz could not resist belittling his rival before the rest of the tribe. This gloating contempt brought him a fierce enemy whose hate would endure down through the years.

Toga-de-Chuz and his new bride settled down on a rancheria on the Gila River. A son was born to them in 1869.

Growing up in close proximity to the white men, the young Apache became friendly with them. The white men simply called him *"Kid"* as they were unable to pronounce his Apache name.

Over the years, his name became *"Apache Kid."* As he grew older, the youth became an expert trailsman, one who stood out even among the Apaches.

Al Sieber took a personal interest in this young man because of this ability to read a trail. When he reached the age of sixteen, in 1885, Sieber enlisted him in Company F of the Apache Scouts. The *"Apache Kid"* rode with troops into Mexico trailing Geronimo at least twice. He also made several forays along and with other scouts. He was with Crook in El Cañon de los Embudos when Geronimo aborted his surrender. The *"Kid"* was with Miles in Skeleton Canyon where Geronimo surrendered on September 4, 1886, after evading five thousand troops for months!

Twenty years after losing the Apache maiden to Toga-de-Chuz, Rip still burned with hate over the scorn and ridicule heaped upon him. He had waited long and with great patience to exact his revenge. Now the time of retribution was near.

The opportunity came at a big Apache "tiswin" party on the Gila River. Rip planted a knife in the heart of his old enemy, then escaped in the furor that followed.

Since the *"Apache Kid"* was the oldest son of Toga-de-Chuz, it was tribal custom that he avenge the death of his father. Otherwise, the Apaches would consider him a coward.

Sieber was away from San Carlos at the time and the *"Kid"* and two of his friends took advantage of this. They rode down to Rip's camp, about forty miles away, to arrest him.

Rip apparently had no intentions of being arrested by an Apache carrying a blood debt and resisted arrest. The *"Kid"* shot and killed him. The three scouts then rode back to their own camp and filled up on Apache liquor.

Later the *"Kid,"* four other scouts, Eskesala, Nin-Kon-Su-Sa, Bosh-lin-ta, Marga, and several agency Indians rode up to Sieber's tent.

Albert Sieber
aka: "Dutchman" and "Iron Man"

Acting Indian Agent Captain Pierce was with Al. When the Agent saw that they were drinking and armed he ordered Sieber to disarm them and put them in the guard house.

Sieber told them to dismount - which they did; he told the *"Kid"* to hand over his rifle and belt of ammunition - which he did.

Sieber ordered the *"Kid"* to disarm the other Apaches and report with them to the guard house.

The *"Kid"* was carrying out these orders and the other Indians had become very excited - when a gun was fired.

It appeared that a dozen Apaches commenced shooting at Sieber at close range.

Still unarmed, Sieber reached inside his tent for his rifle. A rifle bullet hit him in the ankle, shattering the bone.

Author's Note:

"This wound was to cripple him for the rest of his life."

Later, many said that the *"Apache Kid"* shot Sieber, but Al never did. He was positive that a scout called Curly shot him.

The *"Kid"* and his band fled through Arivaipa Canyon, later stealing horses from Bill Atchley's ranch, then killing a prospector, William Diehl, went up the San Pedro where they killed another prospector, William Grace, and then into the Whetstone Mountains on their way to Mexico. However, their escape was cut off by cavalry troops under Lt. Johnson (10th Cavalry), so they turned back toward the reservation.

Johnson and his men killed two of the hostiles and drove them back to the reservation agency, where they surrendered.

Being Army scouts, they were tried by court martial, found guilty and sentenced to the penitentiary at Columbus, Ohio.

A short while later their trial was questioned and it was determined that they should have been tried by a local court. They were pardoned because of a lack of jurisdiction, and released.

About a dozen of them went back to San Carlos by wagon. Company E, 24th Infantry (colored) had their brass band meet them at the Gila River. Hundreds of "agency" Indians went along, too. All of them marched to the Agency behind the music of the brass band.

A great mass of people stood by outside while the ex-prisoners reported to the Indian Agent, Captain John Bullis, 24th Infantry. After reporting they dispersed to various camps.

A move was made to have these culprits re-arrested and retried in the Territorial court. However, they made it a practice to avoid the Agency and stay out of sight.

After awhile they abandoned caution and a troop of cavalry captured them in Agent Bullis' office.

The *"Kid"* and eight other scouts, (Miguel, Say-es, Wash-lan-ta-la, Laccohen, Has-tim-tudo-dy, Ca-do-day-du-on, Pash-lau-ta, and one unknown Tonto Apache), were tried by Judge Joseph H. Kibbey in the U.S. District Court in Globe, for the murder of the freighter. As expected, all were found guilty, and all were sentenced to seven years in the Yuma Territorial Prison.

Author's Note:

"It was a death sentence to an Apache."

Eight Apaches and one Mexican, Jesus Avota, were to be transported to Yuma. In order to transport the prisoners to the Southern Pacific Railroad at Casa Grande Station, a stage had to be taken across the Pinals over a very rough and steep road. They spent the first night at Riverside Station on the Gila River.

From that point the road wound through the foothills, leaving the river. Sand in the road was deep and made progress slow. Being November, the weather was quite cold. The Apaches volunteered to walk to get warm. Sheriff Glen Reynolds, riding horseback by the stage, agreed. Accompanying the Sheriff was a guard, named W.A. "Hunkydory" Holmes, and the owner and driver of the stage, Eugene Middleton.

While going up a steep grade, Sheriff Reynolds was ahead wearing a gun belt and revolver, but with his overcoat buttoned over them. Three Apaches, handcuffed together, came right behind him. Three more Apaches, also handcuffed, followed them. "Hunkydory" Holmes, carrying a shotgun, brought up the rear.

At a signal the three Apaches ahead attacked the sheriff and the three behind fell on Holmes. Reynolds put up a desperate struggle, but could not free his revolver, which was buttoned under his overcoat. The Apaches who felled Holmes snatched his shotgun and killed the sheriff with it. In the midst of all the excitement "Hunkydory" Holmes died of a heart attack.

Middleton, driving the stage ahead of the prisoners, looked back to see what was happening, and took a bullet through the head. He fell off the stage as though he was dead and had the presence of mind to stay "dead."

Taking the sheriffs keys, the Apaches unlocked all the irons, even those of the Mexican prisoner. The latter was terrified, expecting to be killed any moment.

He ran at breakneck speed back to Riverside Station and told what had happened. Word was sent to Florence, and on to Globe and San Carlos by wire.

The news did not surprise Al Sieber, who had tried to warn Sheriff Reynolds about the danger of even being near these desperate prisoners. He had tried to send some of his scouts along—but the sheriff would not allow that. He paid the highest price for his folly.

The escaped prisoners went up the Gila, toward the San Pedro, and by a ranch on the east bank of the San Pedro, a short distance below where Winkleman now stands. They had entered the Cunningham Ranch and when Mrs. Cunningham, who was in the yard, saw them, she had a stroke and died.

Taking to the roughest country to be found, the Apaches left little, if any, trail. Apache Scouts were all over the country looking for them, but never finding them. As long as the *"Kid"* was free, atrocities were attributed to him - some it would have been impossible for him to commit. Still he was blamed and soon a five thousand dollar reward was offered for him, *"Dead or Alive."* Sieber was also given sums of money to hire Apaches for secret assassinations. Often, a stealthy visitor would wake Al in the black of night and whisper a location. Scouts would go to that location the next morning and find a member of the *"Kid's"* band dead by knife wounds. When a body was found as described, Sieber would secretly pay bounty money to the Apache responsible. No one else ever knew who these assassins were and the secret of their identity died with Sieber.

During a Fort Apache tiswin drunk, Josh and Nosey, the latter a well-known medicine man, killed another Apache. Both of these men had been scouts in the Gcronimo campaigns, and they realized that they would be arrested for murder.

Al Sieber knew both men well and realized that they would be invaluable in capturing the *"Kid"* and his band. He had their relatives send them word that if they helped him run down the *"Kid"* he would use all his influence to have them pardoned.

Josh and Nosey were eager to co-operate and immediately started a search for the *"Kid"* or any of his band. They found Pasalau and Sayes on the Gila a few miles from the tiny settlement of Geronimo. Both of these men were battle-hardened, experienced ex-scouts. Josh and Nosey had an ample supply of food and ammunition so Pasalau and Sayes reluctantly joined forces with them.

After several days an opportunity came and, in the fight that followed, Pasalau was killed and Sayes escaped with a number of bullets in him. Josh and Nosey severed Pasalau's head and delivered it to Sieber.

Al kept his word by receiving them as his prisoners then had them pardoned, and then enlisted them in his troop of scouts. Sayes, with multiple bullet wounds, was captured on the Gila. When he had sufficiently recovered, he was sent back to Yuma to serve his original sentence, and died there.

With Pasalau dead and Sayes captured, the *"Kid"* had no more men. Often, he would kidnap an Indian woman and take her into the mountains with him. After about six months, he would release that one and steal another.

The *"Kid"* led a charmed life. No one could seem to corner him. At any rate, he was never captured or killed. He simply disappeared into the mountains of Mexico.

Sieber was laid up for over a year with the shattered ankle. When he returned to duty, he did not get along with Indian Agent Captain John Bullis. Bullis had made a reputation on the Texas frontier by stealing land from peaceful Mexicans.

At San Carlos he started building roads all over the reservation. Labor for this endeavor was provided by Indian prisoners and if there were no prisoners, Bullis made some. He induced the Apaches to spy upon one another. The Indians were sentenced to long periods in the guard house, without being told who had accused them, and without a trial. This was certainly an unfair practice - but it did provide a lot of labor for road-building.

The Apaches were Sieber's friends and this system irked him. It really aggravated him to have his scouts arrest Indians that he knew were innocent.

Finally, Sieber told Bullis straight out what he thought of him and his policies. Bullis fired him and gave him a few hours to vacate the reservation. Sieber moved to Globe and lived there for the next fifteen years.

Al had several gold claims in Del Shay Basin, and some copper claims up on Pinto Creek at Old Cactus Camp. He did his assessment work on these claims and picked up odd jobs. When the building of Roosevelt Dam began, Al was put in charge of a crew of Indians, who were building a new road up to Tonto Basin, the new road to be above the reservoir level.

On February 19, 1907, while the Indians were moving a large boulder blocking the right of way, the rock rolled down the incline.

While Al was trying to get his Indians out of its path, the boulder rolled over him, crushing him to death.

Al Sieber had a high regard for his fellow man and dealt fairly with them all regardless of color. Lonely prospectors and ranchers of the mountains and valleys appreciated him more than any for he was always in the vanguard that provided them protection.

During his service of over twenty years (1871-1891) with the Indian Scouts in Arizona, Sieber served under Generals Stoneman, Crook (twice), Miles, Krautz, Willcox, and Grierson. No one would ever dispute that he was the greatest scout and Indian fighter in the Southwest.

During the campaigns against the Yumas, Mojaves, Tontos, San Carlos, Chiricahua, Hualapias, White Mountain, and the Chemehuevis; all were beaten and brought in.

When word of Sieber's death was relayed to the reservation, there was such mourning from San Carlos to Ft. Apache, that one would believe that a close relative had passed on.

The body was brought to Globe and buried in the G.A.R. portion of the cemetery. The G.A.R. and the Women's Relief Core attended the funeral in a body. While Sieber was lying in state the G.A.R. flag, silk and nine by twelve feet, with long golden cord and tassels was folded and placed on his breast.

The flag was buried with him.

The Territorial Legislature passed the following resolution, which was submitted by George W.P. Hunt and adopted by a unanimous rising vote:

"Mr. President; I desire to offer the following resolution; It has been learned that the slip of a cliff of rocks on the road now building at the Tonto Storage Reservoir resulted yesterday in the death of Al Sieber; late Chief of Scouts under General Crook. And, for thirty years one of the bravest and most efficient servants of Arizona in her Apache Wars. He was one of the bravest scouts ever enlisted and his consul and advice did much to settle the long war with the Indians."

"He held to the day of his death the respect of every Indian who had ever fought with him or against him and the respect and regard of every man or woman to whom he was known. The full measure of his service to Arizona is a story that will never be

told for it is known to no one person, but his name will live as long as we have a history and as long as brave deeds are cherished in the memory of men. I therefore move you that when we now adjourn we do so with expressions of respect for this brave man now at rest, and out of respect to his memory, and that such expressions be embodied in the minutes of this council."

The Council then stood adjourned out of respect to the memory of the late Al Sieber.

So long, "Iron Man."

Pete Kitchen
raised hogs and sold hams and bacon in Tucson and Tombstone.

3

Pete Kitchen
(El Camino De Los Muertos)

During the period 1854–1883 more men were killed between Pete's Potrero Ranch and Magdalena, Mexico than all the rest of Apache territory.

The *Arizona Citizen*, June 1872 wrote:

"He has been on the picket line for 14 years and had buried nearly all his old acquaintances, and should his luck continue he may truly be called the first and last of Arizona's pioneers."

Pete Kitchen would have been the first to say that luck had very little to do with it.

Pete maintained that:

"No man should ever come into this country unless he is willing to kill or be killed. If you give an inch in any way, you are lost. The Apaches have no respect for a coward."

A ceaseless, no-quarter war was waged between Pete and the Apaches. His friends and employees were killed, his stock slaughtered, but there on his land he stayed.

Kitchen was born in Covington, Kentucky in 1822. When he was still quite small, his family moved into Tennessee. Little is known about his childhood.

During the War with Mexico (1846) he was a teamster, moving supplies for the army of General Zachary Taylor. When that War ended, Pete rode west with ten companies of mounted rifles in the capacity of wagonmaster. Their mission was to determine the most suitable locations to establish forts. When they reached Oregon in 1850, he parted with the Army.

Leaving Oregon, he travelled south down to San Francisco and thence to the gold fields for a visit. Apparently, mining and California made little impression upon him.

He went to Southern Arizona about the time of the Gadsden Purchase, late 1853 or early 1854. Settling on Caneo Creek near the Santa Cruz River, he raised and sold beef to the Sonora Mining and Exploration Company, and to the Army.

Kitchen's first ranch home, a one-room adobe

Once, when he was delivering cattle to the Army, the Apaches raided all the ranches in his area. They completely destroyed everything on his small ranch. He had nothing left but his iron will.

Federal troops were sent East when the War Between the States broke out in 1861. They destroyed their forts as they abandoned them.

With the soldiers gone, the Apaches rode where they pleased, murdering, pillaging, and burning as they went. Small settlements and ranches were abandoned; even the Presidio of Tubac. Nothing could stand before the merciless Apache. Anyone foolish enough to travel through southern Arizona during this period saw only burned-out farms and ranches.

His ranch destroyed, Pete went south into Sonora, Mexico and operated a general store in the town of Magdalena. He did well in this venture, returning to the Santa Cruz Valley in 1865. With him he brought a new wife, Rosa Verdugo; her brother Francisco Verdugo; Teresa, Rosa's sister, and her husband, Manuel Ronquillo. This alliance of three brother-in-laws was to endure for many years and through numerous battles.

This time Pete chose some high ground on Potrero Creek close to where the creek emptied into the Santa Cruz River. He had also brought thirty Opata Indians with him from Mexico to serve as farm workers, as well as fighters.

First, they built a one-room adobe hut, where Pete and Rosa resided until they could build more. The others lived in caves in the hillside.

Famous El Potrero stronghold as it appeared, 1915.

—courtesy Arizona Pioneers Historical Society

With the help that Pete brought from Mexico, he built an impressive ranch. The house, sixty feet long, was of adobe, with walls two feet thick, and divided into five very large rooms. Other buildings included a smoke house, blacksmith shop, and a commissary, as well as several barns and storage buildings.

The ranch had about one thousand acres of very rich farming land where fruit, melons, grain, potatoes, cabbages, peppers and tomatoes were raised. He also had large herds of sheep, hogs, and cattle.

Pete had built his home like a fortress, with a four foot parapet all the way around the roof top, complete with rifle ports. The main room of the house was adequately stocked with rifles, shotguns, and an ample supply of ammunition. There was always at least one sentry on the roof and another outside the ranch buildings.

Men, who tended the crops, had rifles swinging from plow handles and every male on the ranch, regardless of age, carned one or more pistols. Pete's house was the safest place on the road stretching from Tucson to Magdalena.

Pete described this roadway as:

"Tucson, Tubac, Tumacacori, To Hell."

Kitchen was described as:

"...the only link between savagery and civilization in Southern Arizona after the Civil War."

Pete's logic was reasonable.

"I'll keep what belongs to me if I have to kill every Apache in the Territory."

He would not appease the enemy and the only way he knew to negotiate was with bullets. He fought them all, the best warriors that Cochise, Victorio, Geronimo and Mangas Colorado could muster. A small cemetery grew in front of the house. It contained the graves of both friends and enemies; ranchers, rustlers, horse thieves, Mexican bandits, Opatas, and Apaches.

Dona Rosa had the workers build a small mortuary close by and it was here that she supervised the funerals and prayed for the dead no matter who they were.

Once, when Pete complained about her prayers for their enemies, she replied, "Even those who are damned have the right of a prayer." No more was ever said concerning her boothill ministrations.

Peace and tranquillity on the ranch would cease abruptly at the sound of a shot. It meant that the sentry had seen Apaches. All the men on the ranch rushed to the house and took up defensive positions. The raiders were always repulsed, but sometimes at a drastic cost. John Rockfellow, a civil engineer, was a close friend of the Kitchen's and often visited at El Potrero. He told the story of a black cowboy that Pete had hired; named Henry.

One day Henry was riding through a deep, rocky canyon when an Apache roped him. Henry quickly grabbed the slack in the rope and took two turns around his saddle horn before the Apache could pull him out of the saddle. This quick thinking action yanked the Apache out of his hiding place and spilled him onto the canyon floor. Henry rode back, lifted the Apache by his hair and cut his throat. Before this incident, Pete had held little regard for Henry, but after it, Henry was always "ace high."

Once when the ranch was under attack, Pete saw an Apache on a rock perched on a hilltop about five hundred yards away. Clearly, the savage thought he was out of range. The Indian bent over baring his backside to Pete and slapping his rear end.

Pete drew a bead on this backside and squeezed off his shot. The heavy bullet struck the Apache at the base of his spine, plowed through the length of his body and emerged through the top of his head. This feat of marksmanship is still discussed in the Arizona country and the rock came to be known as "Pete Kitchen's Rock."

Pete Kitchen's own "Boothill Cemetery."

The Weekly Arizonian on January 24, 1869, stated that all of Pete Kitchen's stock had been killed or run off by Apaches.

Some weeks later the Alta California said that Apaches had killed two hundred of Pete's sheep. It also reported that Abraham Scott who lived at Potrero, was killed and mutilated by the Apaches.

The Citizen on June 17, 1871, reported that Pete's son, eleven years old, had been killed by Apaches about two hundred yards from the ranch. Actually the Kitchens had no son. There was a boy, about four years old, and one about twelve living at Potrero. The younger was Santiago Kitchen and the latter was Fernando Campo.

Pete gave several youngsters a home at his ranch and his name. Five of Doña Rosa's nieces, Rosa, Polonia, Maria, Nieves, and Margarita, also came to live at Potrero. The young victim had been working in the fields and becoming tired, had fallen asleep in a haystack. When the Apache alarm was given, the adults had rushed to the house, forgetting him. The Apaches found him, killed and scalped him. Since it was a boy of about eleven who was killed, it was probably Fernando Campo or *"Crandall"* as some called him.

Pete took great pride in the fine hogs he raised. Estimates of their number range from six hundred to three thousand. His hams and bacon were known all over the Territory. Settlements from Nogales to Silver City were all supplied with ham, bacon, and lard from El Potrero. Tucson stores proudly displayed signs that read:

"PETE KITCHEN HAMS"

The *Tucson Citizen* on June 15, 1872, wrote that during the year he had sold 14,000 pounds of bacon and ham and 5,000 pounds of lard, all of which had averaged bringing him thirty-five cents a pound.

When the Apaches attacked El Potrero, they always hit the hog yard first. They seemed to hate the hogs as much as they did Pete. After every battle, the hogs resembled walking pincushions, they were so full of arrows. The Opatas would remove the arrows from those that could be saved, and kill and butcher those that were badly wounded.

Pete made a business trip to the San Carlos Apache Indian Reservation in the fall of 1875. He was extremely pleased with John Clum's methods as Indian Agent except in one area. There was no whiskey allowed on the reservation. Pete claimed that abstaining for several days in a row was an extreme hardship.

El Potrero was also plagued by horse-stealing bands of Mexican bandits, as it was only six miles north of the border. One night, three of them stole six of Pete's horses and killed one of his Opatas.

Pete took their trail and followed them into Sonora. Locating their camp, he waited until they were asleep, then invaded. He killed one and captured one, but the other escaped.

Returning with his captive, Pete decided to stop for a rest near El Potrero. He put his prisoner on a horse, his hands tied behind him, a noose around his neck, the other end tied to a tree limb. Pete then lay down and took a nap. When he woke up the Mexican was hanging there.

He'd laugh uproariously when he told the story saying, "I never knew that horse to spook before!"

All Pete's neighbors with the exception of one family, the Wrights, had moved on. They considered the *"Road of Dead Men"* too dangerous a place to live.

The Wrights had survived numerous raids and had killed a number of Apaches. When things appeared to have quieted down the old man and his sons made a trip into Tucson, leaving Mrs. Wright and two ranch hands at the ranch.

Cochise's band had just been waiting for such an opportunity. They swooped down on the ranch, killing and scalping Mrs. Wright and the two hands in short order.

The three Wright men returned to this scene of violent death and were so frightened, they fled to El Potrero.

Pete took them in and allowed them to live at the ranch. Some time passed and the men felt it would now be safe to return to their ranch. Still, they were cautious enough to go under cover of darkness. Early the following morning, the Opatas found the three of them, dead and scalped, just beyond the hayfield.

In May, 1871, Lt. Howard Cushing and two of his men were killed by Apaches in the Santa Cruz Valley. Not long after Rees Smith, a neighbor of the Kitchens, was killed by Mexican bandits.

Most of the settlers had either been killed or frightened off at an earlier date.

When the Southern Pacific reached Tucson in 1880, and other rails crossed the whole Territory, Pete keenly felt the competition for his goods. Then, when a railroad paralleled the *"Road of Dead Men"* he knew his time was all over. There would be no more Apaches to shoot or horse thieves to hang.The Apaches even began to avoid El Potrero. They had had enough of Pete Kitchen, his brothers-in-law, and his Opatas. They had whipped the Apaches to a standstill.

Since his time had come and gone, Pete had no more enthusiasm for the ranch. He felt old and tired. He sold out to Colonel Charles P. Sykes. The amount paid for Pete's ranch seemed to be between thirty-three thousand and eighty-five thousand dollars.

In December, 1891, the *Arizona Enterprise* reported that Pete said in an interview the price was thirty-three thousand. His ranch sold, Pete decided to move to Tucson and bought a house there for thirteen hundred dollars.

A few days before they left the ranch, Pete and Francisco stood one last time on the ranch house roof.

"I'm glad that the fighting is over because of the Opatas. So many of them were killed every year." Then, in a voice of complaint, to Francisco, "Them Apaches give up too danged easy. We fight them for twenty-five years, then they up and quit on us."

A final fiesta was held before their departure from El Potrero. The food took three days to prepare; hogs, chickens, and turkeys were roasted; mountains of tortillas were made, as were tamales and many sweet cakes. Pete bought kegs of the finest whiskey that money could buy. Manuel found the best musicians and brought them, to the ranch.

The guests came from Calabazas, Nogales, Tucson, Tubac, and outlying ranches all over the Santa Cruz Valley. Everyone had a great time eating, drinking and dancing. As they grew tired, the women went to sleep in the house and the men in the yard. When it was all over, they sadly bid the Kitchens good-bye. They knew that Pete Kitchen had been their only protection from the Apaches these many years, and that with his going, would go a time that would return no more. All five of Rosa's nieces moved to Tucson with them and their home was still noted for its lavish hospitality. Pete was not careful with his money, never refusing a loan or an investment. It was not long until it was all gone.

Pete died on August 5, 1895, surrounded by family and friends. He had joined the *Arizona Pioneers Historical Society* in 1884, and that organization paid the forty dollars for his funeral and casket.

The *Tucson Star* said the funeral was one of the largest ever seen in Tucson. Pete Kitchen's entire estate consisted of nothing but some household furnishings, which the Probate Court valued at forty dollars, and allowed the family to retain.

Thus ended the life of one of the most remarkable men that ever faced the frontier dangers of the Southwest.

Teresa Ronquillo Masi stands in Pete's cemetery. (Arrow indicates the grave of Santiaguito.)

REFERENCES:

1. A Journey Through Arizona, J. Ross Browne.

2. *Weekly Arizonian,* January 24, 1969.

3. *Tucson Citizen,* June 17, 1871.

4. *Tucson Citizen,* June 15, 1872.

5. *Tucson Citizen,* May 10, 1875.

6. *Tucson Citizen,* October 9, 1875.

7. *Tucson Star,* August 5, 1895.

8. Arizona Characters, by Frank G. Lockwood.

9. Tucson, Tubac, Tumacacori, To Hell, by Gil Procter, 1956.

"Justice Jim" Burnett

4

THE "CZAR" OF CHARLESTON

Charleston actually had its beginning with the Brunckow Mine, which was the first in the vicinity and located a mile north of the site of Charleston. It was never a paying mine, but Ed Schieffelin often stopped there, as early as 1877, while he was prospecting in the Tombstone District.

It was soon after Schieffelin found silver float in the area that he was to name Tombstone. He went West to get his brother to assist him in developing a mine. Richard Gird, an assayer, returned with them. The three of them formed a partnership and opened the door to the Tombstone bonanza.

Gird sold his interest in the Tough Nut Mine in 1879 and with the money, built the Tombstone Mine and Milling Company on the San Pedro River. This was necessary, as Tombstone had very little water in its early silver boom days.

Because of Gird's stamp mill, Charleston came into being. It did not take long for it to grow into a typical boom town where saloons, gambling dens and bawdy houses flourished noisily twenty-four hours a day. Endless lines of heavy ore wagons rolled through the new town carrying the silver wealth of the Tombstone mines to the mills on the river.

Charleston, at birth, was destined to become the most ruthless, wildest and most lawless mining town of the entire West.

The most cold-blooded killers, notorious outlaws, gunmen, thieves and smugglers that an absolutely lawless country could produce walked its streets. Gunfights were so common that the local citizens paid no heed to bursts of gunfire through the night.

It was not unusual to see several dead men sprawled in the street when daylight arrived. Usually, the dead men were buried and no questions asked.

Considering the kind of town Charleston was and its location, it is evident that life from day-to-day was a gamble. Isolated from all civilization, the rough, young town was was in a wild country, infested by fierce Apaches.

Only a few miles south lay the Mexican border, with the country between literally alive with smugglers.

The fantastic silver strike in Tombstone had drawn bandits, crooks of all description, gamblers, prostitutes, gunmen and hawk-eyed killers from all over the world.

True, there was usually a Peace Officer of some sort but, more than likely, these lawmen had been outlaws in the country they had just left, frequently in front of a posse. Consequently, most of the inhabitants of Charleston made their own rules and either enforced them when necessary, or died in the attempt. Gun law was the law of the land and the survivors were the swiftest and most accurate.

It seemed that every killer, gunhawk, rebel and adventurer in the West headed directly for Charleston. Of course, there were the hard-working miners, mill hands, and a sprinkling of settlers, too, but the bad characters greatly out-numbered these good citizens and Charleston was a perfect *haven* for this element.

So this was the setting in 1880: the new camp abounded in badmen, not the least of which was Justice of the Peace, James Burnett, locally known as *"Justice Jim."*

"Curly Bill" Brocius was present as leader of the Galeyville Gang, consisting of rustlers, smugglers, bandits, and murderers. After their

depredations, they relaxed in the saloons and bawdy houses of Charleston. This outlaw leader finally came to his end from a blast of gunfire out of a shotgun wielded by Wyatt Earp.

Two Cochise County Peace Officers, Burt Alvord and Billy Stiles, were also of the badmen stripe. They masterminded a number of train robberies. Arrested, they escaped from the Tombstone calaboose and continued their profitable adventures in crime until Burt Alvord was captured and jailed. Billy Stiles escaped the arrival of justice by fleeing to Nevada.

"Johnny-Behind-The-Deuce" O'Rourke was another would-be badman who acquired his name because he won so much at stud poker, while holding a deuce in the hole. During an argument over such a poker game, the little gambler shot and killed the Charleston smelter's engineer. A constable helped him escape the lynch mob that quickly formed.

They reached Tombstone with the mob right on their heels. The U.S. Deputy Marshal at Tombstone, Virgil Earp, took over and, with his brothers and Ben Sippy, stood off the angry miners. He sent the prisoner on to Tucson for his own safety. However, *Johnny* escaped from the law in Tucson and forever disappeared into the limbo of time and history.

One could correctly say that Charleston was a bad influence in the lives of many a man. Even William C. Greene, one of Charleston's finest citizens, in a fit of temper, murdered an unarmed man, thus establishing himself in the badman group.

Greene went to Tombstone early in the silver boom and built himself a ranch near Hereford. His ranch bordered that of *"Justice Jim"* Burnett.

He gradually invested money in Mexican mines until he had built himself a substantial fortune. Investment intrigued him and he entered into financial ventures in the Wall Street Market. In a short period of time, he had made millions! The money he made he reinvested in the finest cattle land in Arizona and Sonora.

He had first worked as a miner in Tombstone. Then he had cut firewood in the Dragoon Mountains and sold it in *"The town too tough to die"* at fourteen dollars per cord.

Every cent he made, he poured into his ranch at Hereford and the Mexican mining property.

Once Greene had gained control of numerous Mexican mines, he began to build his empire. From it, the Greene-Cananea Consolidated Copper Company came into being.

By 1905, it had developed into one of the leading copper producers, with a settlement of twenty thousand people in the Cananea Mountains of Sonora, Mexico and employing four thousand men in the mines, mills and smelters.

Force, vigor, and violence carried him to success in the wilds of Arizona. He employed the same tactics in the offices of Wall Street.

Because it was known that he would not hesitate to kill an adversary, no one crossed him openly.

On one occasion, he went to an associate's office and, at gun point, took stocks valued at several million dollars. That was the way he would have done it in Arizona and it served well in New York! Though Greene lived his entire life in violence, he died by accident, but that part of the story is for a little later in our quest for *The Legendary Characters of Southeast Arizona.*

"JUSTICE JIM" BURNETT

Of all the characters that may be written about in Charleston during the 1880's, none can surpass *"Justice Jim"* Burnett, the Czar of Charleston.

Although he had crooked tendencies and tactics, he kept the peace as he saw it. One of the most famous stories told about *"Justice Jim"* is the one where he declared Charleston and himself completely independent of the rest of Cochise County.

Immediately after being elected Justice of the Peace, Jim, according to procedure, made out his quarterly report and sent the fines he had collected to the Board of Supervisors in Tombstone. His office was, at that time, a fee office and he was paid for his duties by a percentage of the fines his office took in.

With that quarterly report, Jim billed the county three hundred eighty dollars as his share of the fines from the Charleston District.

Apparently the supervisors felt that this was too much to pay a Justice of the Peace and cut the amount drastically.

Angered at this action, Jim informed the Board of Supervisors that from that time on, the Justice Court of the Charleston Precinct would look after itself. And it did, for never did Jim ask anything of the county nor did he ever send anything. From that time on, Jim kept both the fines and fees for himself, ignoring the county completely.

As the *"Czar of Law"* in Charleston, Jim really worked at his job. There was no red tape to unwind or legal delay in his court. He literally carried the law to the offenders, no matter where he might be. *"Justice Jim"* intended that the court make a good profit and keep busy. If that was not occurring, he stirred things up himself.

His actions were strictly independent and he never asked for help from anyone. Whatever may be said of him, his plans of operation were brilliant; his actions direct and his methods were effective for that time and place.

"Justice Jim" issued his own warrants as needed, then armed with six-gun and scatter gun, served them himself. At any time, any place, and for any reason, he would convene court and dispense justice, immediately!

"Hear ye, hear ye, this honorable court is now in session," were the words often heard throughout the Charleston Precinct.

Burnett took the trial to the defendant; no spot was too inconvenient. His decisions were prompt and his verdicts were enforced by the business end of a six-gun. There was no allowance for appeal and *"Justice Jim"* collected the fines himself. It was uncanny how he could determine to the dollar how much the defendant could pay.

Once a man named Curry filed a complaint that his horse had been stolen. Several days later he recognized his stolen property in a group of horses pulling several wagon loads of firewood. Curry immediately began a claim for his animal. Meanwhile, the Mexican who owned the firewood protested vehemently that the horse was his property.

Jim could always take full advantage of such a profitable situation. He rushed into the street, stopped the argument and declared court in session.

"Is this your horse?' He asked Curry.

When Curry vowed that it was, he ordered, "Take it!"

Then added to the Mexican, "I'll fine you nine cords of wood, delivered to Gird's mill."

Records verify that the wood in the Mexican's wagon measured nine cords almost to the stick!

When such profitable situations did not appear of themselves, Jim was not above creating them.

Once a local saloon keeper got drunk and completely out of control. Jim arrived "Johnny-On-The-Spot" with a constable, Sam Starr. Court was conveniently and immediately convened.

The J. W. Swart Saloon, Charleston

In short order, his Honor declared, "Fined fifty dollars. Court is adjourned."

Jim took the fifty dollar fine, sat in the poker game against the house and in a few hands lost it. However, he had properly and cleverly instructed his constable. That worthy eased over to the saloon keeper and started a noisy argument. *Again* court was convened, *again* the saloon keeper was fined fifty dollars, *again* Jim sat in the poker game, and *again* the fifty dollars was lost. But twice bitten was enough for the saloon keeper even though he was drunk.

When the constable started in his direction he hastily declared it closing time and blew out all the lamps. Meanwhile being extremely careful not to say anything to Jim or his constable.

In another of Jim's cases, Jack Schwartz, also a saloon keeper, shot a man named Chambers. As the victim was a mill foreman, public opinion demanded that action be taken at once. The culprit was arrested and speedily brought to trial.

Jim found him guilty of murder in the first degree and fined him one thousand dollars. Schwartz thought this fine to be a bit high and informed *"Justice Jim"* of the fact. The judge changed the defendant's mind by telling him that a posse from Tombstone was already on its way with a new warrant for his arrest. Schwartz well knew what would be his fate if he was taken to Tombstone, so he hastily counted out the thousand dollar fine, which was promptly pocketed by Jim, while Schwartz disappeared from the vicinity forever.

On yet another occasion, the judge had a similar case in which a Mexican shot a fellow Mexican.

Upon Jim's explicit instructions, a Coroner's Jury rendered the verdict that:

"the Mexican was careless because he stood in front of a gun about to be fired."

Still, he did not pass up an opportunity to profit by the case, as he fined the other Mexican one hundred dollars for "handling firearms in a reckless manner."

Every fourth Sunday, a minister arrived in town to provide church services to the people of Charleston. On one particular Sunday, the meeting place had filled with people and the services had just begun when the doors opened and in walked *"Curly Bill"* Brocius and his

The main street of Charleston, 1882.

entire gang of desperados from Galeyville, all heavily armed.

Sensing that trouble was sure to erupt, the respectable people silently rose and quietly departed. In less time than it takes to tell, the frightened "sky pilot" was left with only the hard cases in his congregation.

Their first act was to fill the collection plate to overflowing, then they demanded a forceful hellfire and brimstone sermon. For several

Charleston, 1885.

—C. S. Fly Photo

hours, they kept the terrified preacher prisoner making him preach, pray, sing, and dance.

Once they tired of this sport, they departed without harming the minister. Though he was exceedingly well paid for his performance, the "sky pilot" never again visited Charleston.

Many of the outraged church members complained to *"Justice Jim"* about the Galeyville gangs' high-handed manner.

Now, not even Jim was about to beard those roughnecks in their own bailiwick, but, to preserve his integrity, Jim did arrest one of the local characters who had been with the outlaws in church.

The culprit was known locally as *"Jaw Bone"* Clark because of his protruding facial bones.

"Court is convened," Jim declared. "The fine is fifty dollars for disturbing religious services."

"Jaw Bone" asked that he be allowed to voice an excuse for being in church and the judge consented.

"I only went to church with the Galeyville gang to keep them from causing trouble there," declared *"Jaw Bone."*

The Judge digested this thoughtfully, then pronounced his verdict, "First charge and fine dismissed. This court now fines you fifty dollars for being in "bad company" on the Sabbath."

"Jaw Bone" knew when he was beaten, and paid the fine.

Although *"Justice Jim"* compromised on occasion, he was definitely not a coward. Jack Haarer once came to Charleston and, after drinking heavily, ran amok, shooting up the town. Running his horse up and down the street, Jack was taking pot-shots at anyone who showed themselves.

Jim ran out, pulled him from his horse and disarmed him. Court was convened on the spot and the badman was fined twenty head of three year-old steers, to be delivered to the Burnett Ranch.

Jim's ranch was well stocked with good cattle from fines that he had levied and from *"finding"* maverick cattle that *"strayed"* from ranches across the Mexican border. By such methods *"Justice Jim"* was on the verge of becoming independently wealthy when fate dealt him the cruelest blow.

William Greene, his neighbor of Wall Street fame and wealth, had built a dam on the San Pedro River in order to obtain irrigation water for his ranch. Scarcely had the structure been completed when it was dynamited. The sudden release of water flooded the entire area below.

Green's young daughter and a playmate were caught and drowned in the flood.

Wild with grief over the loss of his beloved daughter, Greene's crazed mind settled on *"Justice Jim"* as the man responsible for the heinous crime.

Once he had convinced himself that Jim was guilty, he took matters into his own hands. One day he unexpectedly encountered Burnett leaving *"Honest John"* Montgomery's O.K. Livery Stable. Greene's six-gun appeared in his hand and four rapid shots blasted out Jim Burnett's life. Greene rode out of Tombstone toward the border. Marshal White arrested him, but released him on bail.

District Attorney Lord could find but one lawyer who was willing to help prosecute Greene. That man was Colonel William Herring. All the other lawyers in Arizona had been bought by Greene's millions. The accused certainly had no wish to be the guest of honor at a neck-tie party.

It was a costly legal battle, but saved Green's neck. Although it was a clear miscarriage of justice, the jury let him go scot free. It must have cost Greene a fortune to kill Jim Burnett as, for years after, he was known to have still been passing out money to the jurors who freed him.

While Jim Burnett was the dictator *"Czar of Charleston,"* there is no doubt that he committed many crimes and likely aided and abetted or condoned many more. Though guilty of many, he was innocent of the last.

The investigation following his murder proved beyond any doubt that he did not blow up Green's dam. Consequently, he paid the supreme penalty for the one crime he did not commit.

A few sections of adobe walls, disintegrating rapidly under the onslaught of the elements and a few scattered grave markers, are all that remains of the wild boom town.

Hell-raising Charleston is peaceful and quiet. No endless lines of ore wagons roll through the streets. The stamp of the mills is quiet; the saloons and bawdy houses do not exist; the sound of gambling and the cries of revelry are gone; the blast of angry pistols are heard no more.

The buildings that once made this boom town, have disappeared and their inmates have drifted away. Silence reigns, mesquite grows in the streets; the wildest boom town of them all is no more...

REFERENCES:

1. The Czar of Charleston, by Ben T. Traywick.

2. Copper King of Cananea, by Ben T. Traywick.

Bob Paul
One of the Old West's greatest Peace Officers.

5

PAUL
("BOB," THAT IS)

When one describes those that are famous or infamous in the violent past of Southeast Arizona, frequently the names voiced are the Earps, Doc Holliday, Ringo, Curly Bill Brocius, or "Buckskin" Frank Leslie.

Seldom is Bob Paul mentioned, although he was one of the best known peace officers in that part of Arizona's turbulent history.

He was a big man, six feet six inches, two hundred forty pounds, and possessing unbelievable strength. Paul was relentless, determined, brave and totally efficient, probably filling all these categories better than any Arizona Sheriff or U.S. Marshal.

Robert Havlin Paul was born in Lowell, Massachusetts on June 12, 1830. In 1832, his family moved to New Bedford, where the youngster attended public schools until 1842. On July 22, 1842, Paul signed on the whaling ship "Majestic" as Cabin Boy. His first voyage was around the Cape of Good Hope and back by the way of Cape Horn. The voyage was ended with the return to New Bedford on June 2, 1844. The time elapsed was twenty-two months and eleven days.

During this period of time the *"Majestic"* caught fifty-six whales and rendered thirty-two hundred barrels of whale oil. When this oil was sold and the profits divided, Bob Paul received the munificent sum of two hundred fifty dollars for his almost two years of work.

The *"Majestic"* met its end when it was sunk with the Stone Fleet to blockade Charleston Harbor during the War Between the States.

After taking four month's leave at home, Paul signed on another whaling ship, the *"Factor"* on October 1, 1844.

This voyage took him around Cape Horn again and on far into the vast northern Pacific Ocean to Kamchatka on the southern tip of Siberia and to Kodiak on the Aleutian Islands chain.

During September, 1845, while chasing a whale through thick fog and rain in a small boat, the chasers became the chasees. The whale attacked the long boat, completely smashing it, breaking Paul's right leg just below the knee and dumping him into the cold water.

Losing blood and suffering from the cold, salt water, it was an hour before another boat could be lowered from the *"Factor"* and affect a rescue.

Leaving the frigid North Pacific the *"Factor"* sailed to the other end of the world stopping off at New Holland on the coast of Australia in 1846.

From there, the *"Factor"* stood away to New Zealand. Spending considerable time there, they set sail for home in June of 1847.

A hurricane was encountered twelve days after leaving New Zealand's Bay of Islands. This violent storm left the *"Factor"* badly battered, forcing the ship into the nearest port which happened to be Tahiti in the Society Islands. An examination of the ship revealed that it was damaged too badly to attempt repairs and it was condemned.

Bob Paul again shipped out of New Bedford, this time on the "*Nassau.*" This ship spent the remainder of 1847 in the South Pacific and in the Spring of 1848 hove to in the Sandwich Islands for a period of time. They then sailed on to Japan, the Sea of Oshkosh, and into the Artic Ocean, finally returning to the Sandwich Islands in November of 1848. Here, he was paid off by the ship's Captain, leaving Honolulu for America on December 20, 1849.

On February 27, 1849, Paul arrived in San Francisco. Visiting there for a time, he decided to try his hand up in the gold country.

First, he travelled to Hangtown in El Dorado County, staying there until July 3, 1849 at which time he went over to Coloma and participated in their Independence celebration. He did not appear very successful at mining, as he moved on up to the Yuba River country, where he was instrumental in putting the first dam across the Yuba River.

In October, 1849, Paul returned to San Francisco, but did not tarry long there, moving on to Auburn in Placer County. He was moderately successful in placer mining and remained in that area until April, 1850, when he moved to Sierra County in the vicinity of Downieville. Again, he met with some success as he stayed there until October, 1851. Then, for the first time, he visited the camps Mokelumne Hill and Camp Seco, located in Calaveras County.

Paul really liked Calaveras County, but journeyed back to San Francisco in the Spring of 1853. In October of that year, he returned to Camp Seco and took up mining again. He continued at this until he was elected constable in September, 1854. One month later, the Calaveras County Sheriff appointed him deputy sheriff. He served in this capacity until 1857, when he was appointed under-sheriff. With this appointment he moved to Mokelumne Hill.

While serving as under-sheriff, Paul eliminated the notorious Tom Bell Gang that had been operating along the *Mother Lode* for quite some time. Paul had long suspicioned that one Jack Phillips, who ran the Mountain House Hotel between Auburn and Sacramento, was a member of the gang. He proved to Phillips that his real identity as a member of the outlaw clan was known and Phillips told him where the Bell Gang was at that time.

Paul laid an ambush and the unsuspecting gang rode right into it. When called on to surrender, the outlaws elected to go out in a blaze of glory. The posse killed one and captured the others. On the way back they arrested Jack Phillips at Mountain House Hotel. Eventually all the prisoners were tried and sentenced to long prison terms with the exception of the leader, Tom Bell, who was hanged. The complete annihilation of the Bell Gang made Bob Paul the man of the hour in Calaveras County. He became the people's choice for sheriff and won that office by an overwhelming majority in 1859. He was re-elected in 1861 and, refusing to run again, served as sheriff until March, 1864.

He returned to mining in 1865, having accumulated sixty thousand dollars over the years, investing in gravel mining operations.

Nine years later, in 1874, he was completely broke, having lost all his money and his property in unwise mining ventures.

The first Wells-Fargo office in Tombstone, Arizona.

In October of that year he accepted a job with Wells-Fargo and Company as shotgun messenger. This job was to take him into California, Nevada and Utah and lasted until 1877. At that time, the company made him a special detective and sent him to Arizona to investigate criminal activities in the Territory. With his wife and three children, he moved to Tucson. There, he took up his new job with enthusiasm and soon earned the hatred of the outlaw gangs residing there.

By 1880, Pima County Sheriff Charlie Shibell, a very popular Tucson resident, was having monumental problems with six-gun victims all over Southeast Arizona. The *Law and Order Party* selected Bob Paul as their candidate for sheriff.

Wyatt Earp, a Shibell Deputy Sheriff, who had long been disgusted with the way Shibell ran his office, resigned his position and threw his support to Bob Paul. Sheriff Shibell appointed John Behan as the deputy for Tombstone in Wyatt's place. Charlie Shibell won the election over Paul by fifty-eight votes. However, the San Simon Precinct near the outlaw town of Galeyville was under suspicion, with a vote count of Shibell one hundred three and Bob Paul, one.

Paul demanded a recount and in December, 1880, the Board of Elections threw out the ballots from the San Simon Precinct. The judge then declared that Paul had received 1,684 votes and Shibell 1,628 and that:

"...Robert H. Paul was duly elected Sheriff."

Charlie Shibell immediately appealed Judge Frenche's decision to the Arizona Supreme Court which left him as sheriff until the appeal could be decided.

While waiting for the court's decision, Bob Paul put in the time chasing stage robbers in the Globe vicinity and riding guard for the Wells-Fargo bullion stages.

On March 15, 1881, Paul boarded the stage in Tombstone along with driver Eli "Budd" Philpot. The coach was bound for the railhead at Benson. "Budd" was having stomach cramps and it was not long before the two men changed places. Paul had handled the reins before and was glad to spell Philpot for awhile.

Around 10:00pm, with Paul still driving, three men intercepted the stage about six miles from Contention City.

Shots flamed from the darkness on both sides of the coach. Philpot, sitting in Paul's usual seat was hit and fell between the two-wheelers. Paul fired his shotgun at the flashes and put his horses into a run. The outlaws fired at the rear of the disappearing coach and hit Peter Roerig, a passenger. The highwaymen got no loot, but they left two dead men behind them.

Paul was in the posse that chased the killers for over one thousand miles, as were the Earps, and finally captured Luther King. Wyatt Earp and Bob Paul tricked their captive into telling who the other killers were. King named Jim Crane, William Leonard, and Harry Head as his accomplices.

Later that year, on August 25, 1881, a strange newspaper article appeared in the *Arizona Weekly Star.* It read:

"A MYSTERY SOLVED.

"One of the parties recently killed by Mexican regulars in Mexico was the notorious Jim Crane, the last survivor of the stage robbers who murdered Philpot near Benson last spring. From a party who met Crane a few days before his death, the Tombstone Nugget learns the following additional particulars concerning the attempted stage robbery. To many it has always seemed a mystery that the parties mentioned should have killed Philpot and spared Bob Paul, Wells-Fargo Company Messenger. According to Crane, however, when the ambush robbers fired at Philpot, they thought it was Paul, as the two had swapped places, Paul acting as driver and poor Bud as messenger. They meant to kill Paul, thinking that his death would result in the stoppage of the stage, and the easy plunder of Well's-Fargo & Company's box and the passengers. The change from messenger to driver, so Crane says, was made somewhere between the change station and the place of ambush. This he claimed to know as he was the party detailed to watch for the stage, and signal it to his comrades. Why the change was made will probably never be known until the great judgement..... Suffice it that poor Philpot now sleeps peacefully under the daisies, and the intended victim, Paul, still lives, Sheriff of Pima County, and a dreaded terror to the class of whom his intended murderers formed a part."

Author's Note:

"Bob Paul had given the outlaws a great deal of trouble just as a Well's-Fargo employee. Now that he was a staunch ally of Wyatt Earp, they were desperate to keep him from becoming Sheriff."

On his return from chasing the stage robbers, Paul went to Phoenix to hear Shibell's appeal before the Arizona Supreme Court. The judges voted on April 12, 1881, to dismiss the appeal. This order of the Court, Case 479, made Bob Paul Sheriff of Pima County.

Gunfight at the O.K. Corral recreated at the same time, same place, same way as the original—100 years later by Tombstone's famous Wild Bunch–October 26, 1981.

In 1881, Bob Paul rode down to the Indian reservation to quell a disturbance between the whites and the Papagos. The whites had accused the Papagos of stealing their cattle. Not only would the Indians not allow him to make any arrests on their reservation, they held him prisoner for a full day. Paul not only talked the Papagos into freeing him, but convinced them to bring the guilty parties into Tombstone themselves.

A short time after the Gunfight at O.K. Corral, the *"Cowboys"* began to ambush the Earps on the streets of Tombstone, first permanently crippling Virgil then, a few weeks later, killing Morgan.

When they took the crippled Virgil and Morgan's body to Tucson for passage to California, Earp and friends encountered Frank Stilwell and Ike Clanton in the rail yard. They killed Stilwell and Clanton vanished (as usual) when the shooting started.

Warrants were sworn out and Paul travelled to Benson by train to arrest several of the Earp party involved in killing Stilwell.

John H. Behan, the sheriff appointed by Territorial Governor John C. Fremont for the recently created County of Cochise, met him at the train station with a posse of (as Behan described them) *"honest"* ranchmen. The members of this posse were Phin Clanton, Ike Clanton, John Ringo, Frank Patterson, Pony Deal, *"Rattlesnake"* Bill Johnson, Hank Swilling and Harry Woods. When Sheriff Paul saw these *"honest"* ranchmen he refused to ride with them. *The Epitaph* wrote:

> ***"Sheriff Paul, of Tucson, returned to that city. He refused to go after the Earps, because the posse selected by Behan was notoriously hostile to the Earps, and said that a meeting with them meant blood, with no probability of arrest."***

The Earps and Holliday rode out of Tombstone never to return. In New Mexico they sold their horses and caught the train for Colorado. Once there, they wired Bob Paul of their whereabouts. When Sheriff Behan learned their location, he made an attempt to gain custody of the prisoners (after they were disarmed and shackled, of course). However, Governor Tritle placed the requisitions in Bob Paul's hands and sent him to Colorado.

As could be expected, the *"Cowboys"* were very upset at this move, as they wanted Sheriff Behan to have those requisitions. If the Earps and Holliday were arrested, unarmed, and in Behan's custody, they could easily be murdered without danger to their assailants.

The situation being what it was, neither Governor Tritle or Bob Paul had any hope of preventing Behan from gaining custody of the prisoners once they were returned to Arizona. They advised Governor Pitkin of Colorado of the explosive situation in Cochise County and some of the actions of its sheriff. As a result, Pitkin refused the extradition request stating that it was obvious that the charges in the Stilwell killing were pushed solely because it provided an opportunity to murder Earp and Holliday when they were disarmed and unable to defend themselves. Bob Paul returned to Arizona alone.

Paul ran for Pima County Sheriff against Matthew H. Shaw in 1882 and defeated him. His popularity had risen dramatically when he had arrested Tun Hurley for the robbery and murder of an old miner, named Roberts, near Tubac.

It rose again when he arrested Joseph Casey in Calabasas on July 15, 1882, for robbing a man and woman in a house of prostitution. Paul had already arrested a man, named Morton, for murder, and another, named Graham for stealing a horse. He placed all three prisoners in the basement of the Santa Rita Hotel with a guard. Casey broke out that night, but was recaptured in a nearby brick yard.

Paul transported him to the Tucson jail, where he staged another dramatic jailbreak on October 23, 1882. This time he also freed prisoners Gibson, Murphy, Hurley, Moyer, and several others.

El Paso officers captured Casey and notified Tucson. Sheriff Paul went to pick him up and learned that Tim Hurley was in Chihuahua. Leaving Casey under guard, Paul crossed into Mexico and brought Hurley back. By the time he returned to El Paso, Casey had escaped again. He was not recaptured until March, 1883, when he was apprehended in Colorado City.

On April 29, 1883, Casey again made an escape attempt. He obtained a pistol from some unknown source and pulled it on Jailer Holbrook. The jailer tried to retreat and call for help. Casey shot Holbrook in the back. The old man got the door open and yelled loudly for help, then passed out. Guards poured into the jail yard and fired four shots at Casey whereupon he promptly surrendered along with his companion Henry St. Clair.

The jailer died in the hospital late that evening. Citizens of the town made an effort to lynch Casey, but none of them were eager to see Bob Paul use the shotgun he habitually carried.

Both Casey and St. Clair were tried for first degree murder. Casey was tried, convicted and sentenced to hang. St. Clair pleaded guilty to second degree murder and was sentenced to life imprisonment. In 1884, Bob Paul led Casey to the scaffold and hanged him as prescribed by the law.

At the last moment the doomed man yelled, "Good by! Turn her loose!" just as Paul cut the pulley rope.

THE "RED JACK" GANG

It was not unusual for the *"Red Jack"* Gang to hold up the stage between Globe and Florence, but the holdup on August 10, 1883, was different, in that, for the first time ever, they added murder to the charges against them.

They killed Johnny Collins, the Wells-Fargo messenger, then took the treasure box. The gang was composed of *"Red Jack"* Almer, Len Redfield, Frank Carpenter, Joe Tuttle, and Charlie Henslee.

Redfield, Carpenter, and Tuttle were quickly located, arrested, and lodged in the Florence jail. Irate citizens, who had been fond of Collins, stormed the jail, and hanged Redfield and Tuttle. The youngster, Carpenter, was forced to watch. It was a gruesome sight as their necks did not break and they strangled to death. Carpenter was never brought to trial, as he died of nervous prostration before the trial date.

On October 3, 1883, Sheriff Paul received information that the two outlaws still at large, *"Red Jack"* Almer and Charlie Henslee, were hiding out in the vicinity of Willcox. Paul quickly raised a posse and the railroad provided an engine to transport them to Willcox.

The posse encountered the two outlaws at Percy's ranch, about twelve miles from Willcox. In the gun battle that ensued *"Red Jack"* was shot full of holes and killed. Henslee was seriously wounded but, somehow, managed to escape. The Paul posse sustained one slight flesh wound.

Six possemen followed the trail of Henslee, which led toward Point of Mountain. They found him holed up in a dry wash, ten miles from Willcox the next morning. Still full of fight, he fired three shots at Bob Paul, killing his horse. Although he put up a battle as long as he was able to pull a trigger, the posse made short work of him.

It was later learned that both men had taken a vow never to be taken alive. Both were buried in the old Willcox Cemetery.

Matthew Shaw was again Bob Paul's opponent in the sheriff's election of 1884. Paul had been sheriff for four years and was running for a third term. Shaw had many friends and an unlimited financial backing. The sheriff's job was a lucrative plum, as the salary was seven thousand five hundred dollars, plus an additional forty to fifty thousand dollars in fees.Shaw had been campaigning since the last election and it paid off. Paul was defeated by fifty votes. The Election Board counted the ballots and put them in the safe. The Wells-Fargo Agent had sealed the box with his seal. The Board of Supervisors issued a Certificate of Election to Matthew Shaw.

A charge was later made that Paul and his friends broke into the safe and changed enough of the ballots to give Paul the election. They had the Wells-Fargo Agent apply new seals. Judge Fitzgerald, a Republican friend of Paul's, ordered the ballots recounted. This was done and Bob Paul was declared sheriff instead of Shaw.

Democrats O.J. Rouse, Attorney General, and W.K. Meade, U.S. Marshal, called for an investigation and a Grand Jury was called. President Cleveland dismissed Judge Fitzgerald and the latter attempted to dissolve the Grand Jury, but the foreman of the Jury, Tom Jeffords, refused to comply with the judges' order.The investigation continued and Paul remained in the sheriff's office although Judge Barnes declared Matthew Shaw sheriff.

After a year and a half, the attorneys reached a compromise and in July, 1886, Paul relinquished the office to Shaw. The agreement declared that Paul could keep the money he had been paid and that Shaw would serve the last six months of the term.

Paul decided to make one more try at a "big strike" and turned once more to mining, but he was not destined to be a successful miner and wound up broke again.

The Southern Pacific Railroad hired him as a Special Officer in January, 1888.

Three bandits held up a Southern Pacific train at Stein's Pass on Februmy 22, 1888. The bandits were Dick Heart, Larry Shehan, and Tom Johnson, the same men who had been arrested and tried for a train holdup at Pantano in 1887. Unfortunately, they had been released for lack of evidence.

Three separate posses were raised and took the trail of the outlaws who had fled into Mexico. The one led by Bob Paul was successful. He took a train to El Paso and then to Chihuahua City and began the chase from there.

Paul contacted the Mexican officials, who gave him some Mexican soldiers and a Lieutenant to accompany his posse. They intercepted the outlaws near Chihuahua when they took refuge in a ranch house.

Paul set the house on fire and the outlaws came out shooting. The posse and the Mexican soldiers killed all three of them.

The other two posses did not fare so well. One, under Sheriff Matthew Shaw, tired out and returned to Tucson. Another, under U.S. Marshal William Kidder Meade, chose to contact Mexican authorities at Janos some sixty-five miles inside Mexico.

Lieutenant Martinez, Chief of the Customs Section at Janos, arrested the entire posse because they carried no permit of the Mexican Government to enter the country in armed pursuit of criminals. Lt. Martinez held the posse in custody from February 29 to March 23, 1888.

When Republican Benjamin Harrison was elected President in 1888, he appointed Bob Paul U.S. Marshal of Arizona Territory. The citizens of Arizona were extremely happy with this appointment. One Tucson resident wrote Texas U.S. Senator Richard Coke:

"...that no single act of the Senate will prove of such importance to the general welfare of Arizona and New Mexico as the confirmation of Bob Paul as Marshal."

The *Arizona Daily Citizen* said,

"Paul is known throughout the Southwest as a fearless man, who has frequently taken his life into his own hands in the pursuit of criminals."

In the next election the Democrats regained the Presidency, and President Cleveland replaced Republican Bob Paul with Democrat William Kidder Meade in May, 1893.

A short time later ill-health besieged the aging Bob Paul. For many months he wasted away, his giant frame scarcely resembling that of the powerful man he had been.

His obituary, printed in the *Arizona Daily Citizen* on March 26, 1901, read:

"PAUL, ROBERT S.

Robert H. Paul is dead. The end came this morning at 2 o'clock. For months the sufferer had battled with death, his giant strength sustaining him in an effort which was slow to yield to the inevitable death which had marked Bob Paul as a victim. During the last days the sufferer could scarcely talk, and this giant frame had wasted away until there remained but a semblance of the man who was such a familiar figure on the streets of Tucson. As an officer ever working for the suppression of outlawry in the southwest, the character of 'Bob' Paul stands unique, fascinating in its many thrilling memories - a life which was not spent in vain. Knowing not fear, never for a moment feeling the impulse of hesitancy when duty confronted him, brave 'Bob' Paul spent the best years of his life protecting the lives, the homes and property of his fellow men, and now that death has claimed him, all men will bow their heads, friends and enemies alike, and say:

'He was a brave man, and did his duty.'"

"Deceased leaves five children, the mother surviving her husband. The children are: John V. Paul, who is traveling for the International Correspondence School, arrived this morning from Los Angeles; R.J. Paul, who lives in Tucson; Walter and Edith, who live in San Francisco; Edgar who lives at home in Tucson."

"The funeral will be held tomorrow afternoon at 2 o'clock from the residence."

Thus, passed from this mortal coil, Robert Havlin Paul, one of America's greatest peace officers, respected and admired by all who knew him.

REFERENCES:

1. Election Fraud 1880: "The Case of Paul vs. Shibell," by Robert F. Palmquist.

2. Arizona Historical Society, Robert H. Paul Biographical file, Tucson.

3. *Arizona Daily Citizen.*

4. *Doc Holliday,* by John Myers.

5. *Arizona Republican.*

6. *Sheriffs' Magazine,* James Barney, February 1949.

7. United States Marshals of New Mexico and Arizona Territories 1846-1912, by Larry D. Ball.

John Harris Behan
First Sheriff of Cochise County, Arizona

6

JOHN H. BEHAN

FIRST SHERIFF OF COCHISE COUNTY

John Behan was born in Westport Missouri on October 23, 1845. His parents Peter Behan and Sarah Ann Harris had a total of fourteen children. Not much is known about John's childhood except that he received an above normal education for that period.

John seems to have had serious difficulty in dealing with the problems along the Kansas–Missouri border in those years. Apparently, even his mother and father had opposing views on the slavery issue. Therefore, young Behan got away from it all by heading West in 1863; first to San Francisco, then to Prescott in Arizona Territory.

His obituary in the *Arizona Sentinel* states that:

"...he made an enviable record as a daring rider for the Pony Express, carrying mail on mule or horseback between Prescott and Phoenix. It is said of him that he was one of the fastest and surest riders of the southwest and was known to make as high as 132 miles in one riding, evading, fighting, or outrunning Indians whenever they crossed his path."

Author's Note:

"This doesn't sound like the real Behan, and if it is, he certainly wasn't doing it for the Pony Express."

As early as 1866, he was written up as being involved in skirmishes with the Apaches. Late that same year, he was appointed deputy sheriff. In 1867, he became under-sheriff of Yavapai County.

Behan resigned his office in March, 1868, and ran for the office of county recorder to which he was elected in June.

In March of 1869, he married a woman named Victoria Zaff in San Francisco. They were to have two children, Henrietta born in 1869, and Albert in 1871. Henrietta died while very young.

Apparently, young Behan was a brilliant politician, as he was elected sheriff of Yavapai County in 1871. After serving his term as sheriff, John freighted for the mines with bull teams.

In 1873 he ran for and was elected to the Seventh Legislature Assembly. By May of 1878, Behan had moved to Signal and was running for sheriff there. It was one of the few times he was not victorious in the political arena. He did win a seat in the Tenth Legislative Assembly (Mojave County).

Behan left Prescott in October, 1879, to accept a job in Gillet as deputy sheriff. It was while he was with a posse from this office chasing Mexican stage robbers that he met the person who was to drastically change his life: *Josephine Marcus.*

The young lady from San Francisco had run away from home to join a traveling show. Behan escorted the troupe into Prescott.

Josephine returned to Tombstone in 1880 where John worked in the Grand Hotel. He had lured her to Tombstone with a promise of marriage. Josie moved into the house with him, but the marriage never materialized.

Josephine Marcus.

Behan soon began to expand his business interests and took John Dunbar as a partner to open the Dexter Livery Stable.

Wyatt Earp and his brothers had come to Tombstone in late 1879 and Morgan (another brother) arrived in the summer of 1880. Wyatt and John Behan were destined to become rivals for Josie Marcus as well as in the political field.

In July, 1880, Sheriff Charlie Shibell appointed Wyatt as a Pima County Deputy Sheriff. Wyatt's brother, Virgil, had been appointed a U.S. Deputy Marshal by Marshal Crawley Dake back in November of 1879. Fred White had been elected Tombstone's first town marshal on January 6, 1880. Alder Randall was the mayor.

On October 27, 1880, the *"Cowboy"* gang was involved in shooting-up Allen Street. Marshal White and Deputy Wyatt Earp set out to disarm them. White encountered *"Curly Bill"* Brocius on the lot where the Bird Cage Theater now stands.

When told to surrender his weapon, *"Curly Bill"* extended it barrel first. White grasped the barrel and the pistol fired. Shot through the abdomen, White fell, writhing in agony.

Wyatt Earp pistol-whipped *"Curly Bill"* rather severely and threw him in jail. White lived a few days, then died.

"Curly Bill" was tried, but the shooting was defined as an accident and he was freed.

Mayor Randall appointed Virgil Earp marshal to replace White on October 28, 1880.

Charley Shibell was opposed by Bob Paul in the upcoming election for sheriff. As a close friend of Paul's, Wyatt could not support Shibell. In view of this, he resigned as deputy sheriff. John Behan was appointed to replace him.

A demand for the creation of a new county began to push the legislators in that direction. News soon became known that Cochise County would be formed from a portion of Pima County on February 1, 1881.

As that date was approximately midway between elections, the people who would run the new county until the regular election would be appointees.

The sheriff of the county was a very much desired position, as he was also the tax collector, and as such would receive a percentage of the taxes he collected.

Wyatt wanted to be sheriff and felt he was well qualified. He had already held several positions as a lawman. He, the Territorial Governor and Government were all Republican, but the Democratic machine held power in Tombstone. Another man desired the office of sheriff: *John Behan.* He also had political connections and was a glib politician; something that Wyatt was not. It was just a guess as to which man would get the job until Behan approached Wyatt with a *"deal."*

The *"deal"* Behan made was that if Wyatt would withdraw and let him be named sheriff, then he would name Wyatt as his under-sheriff and next year in the regular election, he would withdraw and let Wyatt have a clear field to run for sheriff.

They made an agreement to that effect and Governor Fremont appointed John Behan as Cochise County's first Sheriff when the new county was created on February 1, 1881. However, when the time came, Behan reneged on his agreement with Wyatt and named a Democrat, Harry Woods, as his under-sheriff.

Virgil Earp had run for the office of town marshal in January, 1881, but lost because he had made himself unpopular with several rather strict ordinances that he had proposed to the City Council and then rigidly enforced when they were passed.

Ben Sippy won the job, but by June, he had had enough. He applied for and was granted a leave of absence. He must have considered the job too much to handle and the town too tough, for he didn't return, but conveniently disappeared.

Morgan S. Earp

—Glenn Boyer collection

When John P. Clum, now the mayor of Tombstone, realized Sippy was apparently not coming back, he called a meeting of the City Council and appointed Virgil Earp to replace Sippy on July 4, 1881.

When the J.D. Kinnear Stage had been held-up back in March of 1881, driver Eli "Budd" Philpot and posse captured one of the outlaws, Luther King, but Behan and his cronies allowed him to escape. Then they tried to implicate Doc Holliday, an Earp friend, in the hold-up and murders. This charge was thrown out.

On the night of September 8, 1881, the Bisbee Stage was robbed. Pete Spencer and Frank Stilwell were arrested for the robbery. Stilwell was a deputy of Sheriff Behan's as well as his partner in a Charleston livery stable. Matters reached a climax on October 26, 1881.

Wyatt Berry Stapp Earp
—Glenn Boyer collection.

That morning, Ike Clanton came to town and was roaming the streets of Tombstone, armed and boasting that he had come to kill Earps. Virgil pistol-whipped him and dragged him down to Justice Wallace's Court, where he was fined and released.

Outside the court, Tom McLaury made the mistake of challenging Wyatt, who hit him over the head with his gun barrel and left him lying in the street.

Early that afternoon, word came to Virgil that the *"Cowboys"* were down next to Fly's Photography Studio and still armed. Virgil, Wyatt, Morgan, and Doc Holliday, confronted the *"Cowboys."*

Sheriff Behan always claimed that he tried to disarm the *"Cowboys,"* and perhaps he did try. If he did, he certainly wasn't very successful.

THE GUNFIGHT AT O.K. CORRAL

As could be expected, the confrontation developed into a full-scale gun battle.

Billy Clanton, Tom and Frank McLaury were killed and Virgil and Morgan Earp were seriously wounded.

The *"Cowboy"* faction retaliated swiftly with an ambush of Virgil Earp, crippling him for life. A few weeks later Morgan was shot to death while playing a game of pool.

When Wyatt was in Tucson to send the crippled Virgil and Morgan's body to Colton, California, he spotted Frank Stilwell in the train yard.

Wyatt and his friends filled Stilwell with buckshot and left him dying.

In a few short days Wyatt, now a Deputy U.S. Marshal, and his federal posse, accounted for the deaths of Florentino Cruz, *"Curly Bill"* Brocius, and Johnny Barnes.

Meanwhile, Sheriff Behan was running about the country, presumably *(to hear him tell it)* trying to find Wyatt and his friends. Yet, every time he was told of their whereabouts, he always seemed to ride in an altogether different direction.

Warrants had been issued for several of the Earp party involved in the killing of Stilwell. Bob Paul, sheriff of Pima County, rode the train to Benson to make these arrests.

Sheriff Behan met him at the train station with a posse of, *(as Behan described them), "honest"* ranchmen.

When Sheriff Paul saw these *"honest"* ranchmen, he refused to ride with them.

Wyatt and Doc Holliday disappeared from Arizona and reappeared in Colorado. Behan tried every avenue to have them extradited and remanded into his custody.

Governor Pitkin realized that, to do so, would result in the murder of Wyatt and Doc, so he refused to allow extradition.

With his enemies gone, Behan had things his own way- until election time. He lost the election for sheriff to Jerome L. Ward.

His outlaw posse had shaken his own party so badly that they gave him little support. Things got worse. Behan was indicted by the Grand Jury for a mistake in his accounts and for collecting taxes after Ward became the legal Sheriff and Tax Collector.

The *Phoenix Gazette* dated November 28, 1885, reports:

"Two of the Territorial Prison Commissioners bave resigned, and it is reported that Superintendent Ingalls will follow their good example. In this event the Gazette would like to see Johnny

Behan, of Cochise County receive the appointment. Having been sheriff in Yavapai, Mohave, and Cochise counties, he has had a training particularly fitting him for the position. His ability and Democracy are unquestioned, and we know of no man in the Territory who would fill the place as superintendent of the prison more satisfactory."

On October 1, 1887, John Behan was appointed, by the Board of Prison Commissioners, to the position of assistant superintendent to fill the vacancy caused by the resignation of Joseph Cottreal.

On April 1, 1888, he was appointed Superintendent of the Territorial Prison to fill Superintendent Thomas Gates' place, upon his resignation.

A Presidential election ended this job for Behan on July 5, 1890. When President Cleveland went out of office, so did Behan. The only man that John Behan ever killed was during an attempted prison break while he was employed at the Territorial Prison.

The records from the prison state that John was living in Philadelphia on October 31, 1891. This information was from a private letter and did not reveal what Behan was doing there.

On April 16, 1892, the *Arizona Sentinel* reported that Behan and a man, named Ed Jones, had formed a partnership and had recently gone into the commission business in Washington, D.C.

In June, 1893, he was appointed Inspector of Customs in Buffalo, New York. By September, he was holding that position in El Paso.

His job as Inspector of Customs was terminated in March, 1894. Evidently, he did not take long to find employment as an Arizona paper reported on September 8, 1894:

"John Behan, Chinese Inspector of Texas, New Mexico, and Arizona, came in on Tuesday evening's passenger from California and remained over one day. Wednesday he continued his journey to Nogales."

The *Tucson Star* on May 8, 1897, wrote:

"It is said that Chinese Inspector J.H. Behan is now a private citizen, the office having been discontinued or he having resigned. It is generally admitted that Mr. Behan made a very acceptable official."

When the Spanish-American War broke out Behan served as a civilian quartermaster with the Army working for Brigadier General C.F. Humphrey. He can be placed in Cuba in May, 1898, and until the summer of 1899.

Still in the quartermaster service and still working for General Humphrey he went to China in August, 1900.

McClintock states that,

"Behan saw active service at the front in Cuba and took part in many engagements during the Boxer uprising."

Author's Note:

"This author can find no record of any "combat" by Behan in Cuba or China. He was a civilian employee and they are seldom sent to the front in any war."

Back in America, Behan tried politics one more time. He ran for sheriff at El Paso but was defeated in the primary in 1908. Much of his remaining years were spent in Tucson where he was the head of the commissary department of the Arizona Eastern Railroad.

He was working in this capacity when death took him at St. Mary's Hospital in Tucson, on June 7, 1912. His death was caused by hardening of the arteries and acute Bright's Disease. John is buried in an unmarked grave in the Catholic section of the Evergreen Cemetery in Tucson.

REFERENCES:

1. *Real West Annual,* Assistant Folk Hero, by Glenn Boyer, Johnny Behan: Spring 1983.

2. Yuma Quartermaster Depot, Arizona State Parks, Yuma, Arizona.

3. I Married Wyatt Earp, by Glenn Boyer: University of Arizona Press, 1976.

4. The O.K. Corral Inquest, by Alfred Turner: Creative Publishing Company, 1981.

Bronze plaque installed at the grave of John H. Behan by the Tombstone Wild Bunch, 1990.

Crazy Horse Lil'
She would fight men or beast!

7

A Woman's Choice: Suicide or Scandal

It was really a shame! All those girls gone bad. We are referring to those women of the West, who followed the boom towns, practicing the world's oldest *"profession."* Of course, these women were called *"sinful"* but then, again, some of them really had *no* other choice.

In those difficult times, there were no food stamps, welfare, or any other Government assistance programs. Each individual was compelled to accept the responsibility for his or her own life, survive or not.

The men of that time were rugged and independent individuals and most found a way to survive, however, a woman of that period was in dire need of a man, either father, brother, or husband to take care of her with very few exceptions.

There were few jobs open to women; i.e., seamstress, cook or laundress and jobs, such as these, paid only survival wages.

Conditions then forced many young women with no man to take care of them, to make a choice between suicide or scandal. Many boothills of the West contained the remains of those who chose suicide, but the *"Red Light Districts"* claimed a fair share of them, too.

Those who chose this line of endeavor were assured of survival, at least for awhile, and with an above-average income. True, it was a tough existence, but better than ending it all and those women who were rugged and independent enough survived this way.

Most women quickly discovered that men greatly out-numbered the women, and that any female who had a smile and pleasant personality and showed a spirit of co-operation in bestowing her sexual favors, could name her own price for those favors.

It would be truthful to say that the people who were welcomed most in the wild mining camps were the "Red Light" women. Some of them were part-time entertainers, hoping to strike it rich; others were simply ladies of joy, who enjoyed their work, trying to make enough to retire before age thwarted them; others were prostitutes because they saw no other avenue to survival; and others were just mercenary.

Naturally, the men welcomed the arrival of these *"Painted Ladies"* with wild celebrations. Their presence and fancy houses added a bit of refinement to the rough camps. The women, themselves, offered pleasure, amusement, and companionship to the lonely men, as it was usually some time before the respectable women began to arrive.

Many of the more attractive prostitutes worked as performers at local theatres and dance halls. Older and less attractive *"Ladies of Joy"* worked in cribs, on the street, or in the saloons where they caged drinks from the customers, and for which they were paid a percentage.

The girls would entice customers to buy a drink for them, ordering whiskey, and the mark would pay for whiskey, though the drink was really tea.

Usually there were two types of dwellings that served as *"Houses of Ill Repute."* The crib and the fancy *"Parlor House."* Strangely, they were located in the same neighborhood and sometimes, side by side.

The cribs were simply tiny buildings, usually ten feet by eight feet in size and constructed of rough lumber. Furniture usually consisted of one straight-backed chair, a tiny table on which a washbowl sat, a single iron bed, a bottle of carbolic acid, and a small trunk for clothing. An oil cloth was usually spread over the bedclothes.

A customer, who sought the low prices of the cribs, was certainly not allowed to take off anything but his hat, and the oil cloth was to protect the bed clothes from his boots.

Rent, on accommodations such as these, cost the prostitute about three dollars per day, paid in advance. This small area was where she lived as well as where she conducted her business. Cribs were the lowest and most disreputable places to work. Prices for these women were set in a strange pattern.

Mexican:	$ 0.25
Chinese, Japanese, Negro, and Indian:	0.50
French:	0.75
American:	1.00

These prices would change depending on age, beauty, or special abilities. Usually, these women wore nothing but high heels. On a mine payday night, a girl could entertain eighty to one hundred men.

Most parlor houses were at least two stories, sometimes more. The lower floor was usually a saloon where a man might drink, dance, and gamble as much as it pleased him.

In the upper parlor or parlors, girls and rooms were available for those who tired of the entertainment on the first floor, at a price, of course.

The inside was elaborately and lavishly decorated, with carved furniture, red velvet drapes, full length mirrors, exotic paintings, and deep, soft rugs. Young, attractive maids and a uniformed butler served the customers on the first floor.

"*Parlor Houses*" had a standard fee that was about ten dollars. Young and beautiful girls could demand higher prices. So could the older women who had special skills or a well-known passionate ability.

Each house had up to thirty girls. An ambitious prostitute in a popular house could realize one hundred fifty dollars per week (very high wages for that time). Hours of operation were usually from noon to daybreak each day.

The girls had one day a week off. One big profit maker for a *"Parlor House"* was beer, whiskey, and champagne. Customers paid one dollar for a beer or a pony of whiskey, three dollars for Mexican wine, and five dollars for a bottle of champagne.

In order to have a quiet and refined business, there were some madams, who sold no alcohol of any kind, tolerated no profanity, had no gambling, and allowed none of their girls to touch or be touched except behind closed doors. One strict rule was always rigidly enforced:

"Payment in advance."

When a customer entered a house, all the available girls lined up for his inspection, after which, he would make his choice.

Sometimes, the girls were dressed in filmy underwear or in transparent dresses with nothing underneath.

All the houses allowed their girls to hand out business cards. Most of these cards had only the girl's name and the house's address. Others carried "starting" information, i.e.:

"Elderly gentlemen, ask for Maxine. She is adept at coping with matters peculiar to advanced age."

Some houses allowed the girls to sell photographs of themselves totally nude and in rather unusual poses. This was discontinued at the first complaint by the police.

In the parlor of every house there was a sign which read:

When an obviously easy mark appeared, the entire personnel of the house would endeavor to help separate him from his money. They held a *"virgin auction"* in which he was allowed to participate.

The auction was held in the *"virgin's"* room, in the center of which, stood a huge brass bed decorated with ribbons and flowers.

Walls and ceiling were covered by huge mirrors. The drapes were red velvet.

In almost all cases the *"virgin"* was a prostitute, who looked young and could act enough to appear reluctant, frightened, and innocent. Only the most inexperienced customer could be taken in by this hoax. Still, the rewards were worth the effort as sometimes the girl would bring ten times the *"all night"* price.

Women of the *"Red Light District"* were of various races and nationalities including American, Mexican, Chinese, French, Negro and Indian. Records indicate that the-most successful prostitutes were red-headed, with blondes close behind. Most men really believe that women with red hair are much more passionate than other women.

American girls, who served the *"Houses of Ill-Repute"* in the West, were usually from small towns.

Pimps enticed them to leave home with them, then either sold them to the houses or received a percentage of the money the girls earned.

French girls were hired by syndicates or prostitution rings and transported to the western camps.

Chinese girls were purchased as property, like cattle and shipped to America. They were owned, sold and traded. Tongs usually owned two or three thousand Chinese girls and shipped them to mining towns all over the West.

Most Chinese considered female children as worthless and drowned them if they could not sell them. A girl of fourteen, (which was considered the best age for prostitution) with beauty and grace, would bring a price up to one hundred dollars in China. Upon her arrival in California she was worth one thousand dollars or more. In Tombstone, she was worth fifteen hundred to two thousand dollars.

Chinese prostitutes in the *"Red Light District"* would try to attract customers by baring their breasts before windows.

They would call out,

"Look-ee! Feel-ee! Do-ee! Six-bit-ee!"

These Oriental prostitutes were in great demand in the isolated mining camps, chiefly because the laborers and miners had been told that the anatomical difference between white women and Chinese women was so startling that it was unbelievable. They would pay huge amounts of money to prove to themselves that there was not a difference.

Some would return two or three times to assure themselves that they had not been mistaken in what they saw.

Some of the fancier houses had colorful signs outside. They and the cribs boasted a red lantern by the front door, dusk to dawn.

All the *"Fallen Angels"* were required to have a medical certificate which was obtained by submitting to a medical inspection each week.

Most of the girls in Tombstone went to Dr. Goodfellow. One Tombstone Marshal made all the *"working girls"* have a photo made and given to him. Any girl, who was found to be diseased, was not allowed to continue her *"profession"* until she had been treated and pronounced cured by the doctor.

When respectable women came to the camps, they completely ignored the existence of the *"Red Light"* women. They never, never referred to the cribs or houses as brothels, bordellos, or cribs, they were *"Female Boarding Houses."* After all, it did sound more civilized and refined to refer to Mrs. O'Hara and her *"girls"* than to say *"Soiled Doves"* in cribs.

This farce was continued in the manner that since the *"girls"* were single they were, therefore, *"virgins"* and the men, who frequently visited them, were "*Gentlemen Callers,*" keeping them company.

Most all the early camps allowed for prostitution and even made money from it. A license was sold to allow the woman to operate. The money from the sale of these licenses was the sole source of revenue for schools in Southeast Arizona for a long while.

An area was most always set aside by local ordinance where the women could live and conduct business with their activities controlled.

"Professional" ladies were restricted from any form of public solicitation except in these designated areas, the dance halls and the saloons. Quite often the streets which served as home and work place to these women were labelled *"Virgin Alley"* or *"Maiden Lane."*

What the camp fathers were doing with the restrictions on the activities of these women and the polite, rather than blunt, words, was appeasing the generally proper, respectable women and ascertaining that they would not be offended.

Many a *"Lady of the Line"* and or bordello madam became angels of mercy during times of crisis in the mining camps. Some of the first class houses were palaces in their grandeur.

When epidemics (scarlet fever, diphtheria, smallpox, plague, influenza, etc.) struck a camp, there was no place to put all the people stricken by the illness.

In almost all cases, the madam would convert her *"palace"* into a temporary hospital and she and her girls would minister to the sick and comfort the dying until the epidemic had run its course.

A large number of the fund raising events would not have been successful without the help of the *"Red Light"* women.

Blonde Marie

Dutch Annie

Tombstone, as an example, got its Episcopal Church built through money donated by gamblers, saloon keepers, and the *"Houses of Ill-Repute."*

Although they were the first to contribute to worthy causes, the women from the *"Houses of Ill-Repute"* also used this opportunity to get even with the respectable women.

This is how one woman from the Bird Cage exacted her revenge, told in her own words:

"The women from uptown always looked down their noses at us, excepting when they needed some money for a charity. Then, they'd come down and ask us girls. Well, I always donated, but I got my kicks in doing it. I had found out from a old lady that if you used a certain size coin and placed it just right, then you wouldn't get pregnant (forerunner of the diaphram). Well, when I used them coins, I laid them on the table in my room. Then, when them society ladies come down for a donation, I give them the coins on my table."

Respectable ladies referred to the contributions of the *"Red Light"* women as *"guilt money"* but their generosity was seldom, if ever, refused. Even though the society ladies wanted to get rid of the *"Houses of Ill-Repute,"* they could not deny the good they did when needed.

Most of the *"Scarlet Ladies"* were known by nick-names, seldom ever revealing their real name. This was because they didn't want their family to know about them and if they ever had the opportunity to become respectable, then no one would ever associate them with their real name.

"Houses of Ill-Repute" have always been a significant part of Western history; though not all of them have been worthy of praise. However, the girls who found them their only means of survival, made the best of their circumstances and most tried to be good citizens of the West.

In any event these lusty, busty women were a part of the settling of the American West, equally as important as the prospectors, gamblers, and ranchers.

Many a man had the *"Ladies of Sin"* to thank for the stake that started them.

Ordinance No. 31

The Mayor & Common Council of the City of Tombstone, Territory of Arizona, do ordain as follows.

That section 64 of Chapter 17 of the Code of ordinances of the City of Tombstone. approved August 30th 1881 be amended to read as follows

Sec. 64 - Every person keeping a house or room of Ill Fame in which one or more persons are inmates, shall pay a monthly license of ten dollars, & every person keeping such house where wine, malt or spirituous liquors are sold, shall pay a monthly license of twenty dollars.

S. B. Chapin
Clerk

V. A. Gregg
City Attorney

Approved December 8th 1881
John P. Clum
Mayor

John P. Clum
Mayor

Attest
S. B. Chapin
Clerk

REFERENCES:

1. *Tombstone Tumbleweed,* Good Girls Gone Bad, by Jim Spencer.

2. Hell's Belles of Tombstone, by Ben T. Traywick, Red Marie's Bookstore, 1984.

3. Chinese Dragon in Tombstone, by Ben T. Traywick, Red Marie's Bookstore, 1989.

GLOSSARY

Names Applied to Prostitutes:

Scarlet Ladies
Painted Ladies
Calico Queens
Shady Ladies
Ladies of the Night
Hookers
Love Goddesses
Soiled Doves
Fallen Angels
Hell's Belles
Ladies of Sin

CHINESE:

Lotus Flower
Daughter of Joy
Celestial Lady
Kimono Girl

Allen English

8

Allen English
Rotten Row's Finest

There are many fascinating tales told of the characters who inhabited the area on Fourth Street between Allen and Toughnut Streets in Tombstone during the 1880's. This short stretch of street bore the unbelievable name of *"Rotten Row."* The buildings here were one-story adobes, weather-stained and eroded by the elements.

The characters inhabiting *"Rotten Row"* were the attorneys who handled Tombstone's legal matters. They were quite content with the location of *"Rotten Row,"* as they considered it ideally situated near the courthouse and a saloon. Actually more legal cases were settled in the saloon than in the courthouse.

At any rate, the legal *"lights"* spent a great deal of their time traveling between the two.

The best of these (the most talented lawyer Tombstone ever had) was Allen R. English. He was a man of humor as well as an artistic persuader of judge and jury. But, as many another good man, his downfall was brought about by *John Barleycorn.*

English was born in Saginaw, Michigan; in the year 1860. At twenty, he arrived in *"The town too tough to die"* and went to work in the silver mines.

Shordy after his arrival, he attracted the attention of Marcus Aurelius Smith, a well-known lawyer and congressman. Impressed by this unusual young man, Smith made him a junior partner in the law firm of Smith and Goodrich. English moved into his newly acquired office with his unbelievable wit, his law book and a bottle of good bourbon.

On one occasion English appeared to defend a client in the court of Judge George Davis so intoxicated, he could scarcely stand. Angered at such a display by one in the legal profession, Judge Davis fined him twenty-five dollars for contempt of court.

With the assistance of a sturdy chair, English rose to his feet and yelled, "Your honor, twenty-five dollars won't pay for half the contempt I have for this court!"

More often drunk than not, English always made a fantastic appearance in Court. He was an excellent lawyer, drunk or sober, and perhaps a little better when *"under the influence."*

With an unusual ability to consume an unusual amount of liquor, he readily drank with friend and foe alike at any occasion.

Once, while totally and completely inebriated, he successfully defended Wiley Morgan. Morgan, a participant in the Earp-Clanton feud, had shot a man and the County had charged him with murder. English had attempted to convince the jury to change the charge to self-defense.

When the judge declared the court adjourned for lunch, English hurried to Billy King's Saloon to clear his throat. By the time court reconvened he had imbibed too much and lay on the saloon floor completely unconscious.

Billy King took him back to the courthouse in a buggy from the O.K. Corral. It required two strong men to usher the wobbly English into the courtroom. Drunk as a lord, he made his final appeal to the jury and, as it was the best he'd ever made, cleared Morgan.

Once, during his law career, the Santa Fe Railroad offered him the job as their head attorney, at an unheard of twenty five thousand dollars a year. However, they did ask English to agree that he would quit drinking.

"What?!!" he yelled, livid with rage. "Give up my rights?!" "Hell, no!" And he didn't!

In addition to all his other numerous talents, English was evidently one of the better actors of the period. At will, he could send large tears coursing down his cheeks.

In turn, he could reflect any mood necessary to sway judge or jury; he could be serious, demanding, indignant, outraged, sentimental, ironic, sarcastic, or poetic, as the need arose.

Lawyer English demanded and received fantastic fees for his services. When the Irish Mag in Bisbee was sold, the new owners hired him to check the title papers. English complied and sent them a bill for twenty-five thousand dollars, an amount completely unreasonable.

In some way, he had acquired several shares in the Black Diamond Copper Mine near Pearce. At the opportune moment, he put his holdings up for sale and picked up eighty-four thousand dollars. He used these same tactics to make eighty thousand dollars from the Emerald Silver Mine in Tombstone.

Although he made fantastic sums of money, English seldom managed to keep any of it. With the proceeds from the two mining ventures, he and his wife took a trip East. When they returned after several months of high living, he was flat broke. All of English's problems seemed to be because of drinking.

Once, in the midst of a murder case in Judge Alfred Lockwood's Court, he requested a recess. During the time granted, he scurried to a nearby out-house and drank an entire bottle of bourbon that he had hidden there earlier. By the time court went into session, his speech was slurred and he staggered noticeably.

Because of his condition, the Judge recessed court until the following day after, reprimanding English quite severely, warning him never to appear in his court under the influence of alcohol. English solemnly promised that there would never be a reoccurrence. Still, on the following morning, he staggered into the courtroom drunker than ever. It was apparent that he had spent the night with the bottle.

"Council English," thundered the Judge in anger, *"I warned you concerning your behavior in this courtroom yesterday and you have ignored me and your promise! I hereby sentence you to thirty days for contempt of this court!"*

For the following fifteen minutes, the judge and court were subjected to English's speech in which he quoted the Bible, Shakespeare, Greek and Latin poets, motherhood, and the Pilgrims. Judge Lockwood and individuals in the courtroom let tears roll unchecked and unheeded at the unparalleled eloquence of a drunken lawyer.

At last the judge could stand no more. "Enough, Mr. English, enough. I hereby reduce your sentence to fifteen days."

As he was led from the courtroom, English remarked to a friend seated nearby, "Well, I talked my way out of *half* of it anyway."

English went to jail on the contempt charge, but served only a part of his sentence.

He made such a nuisance of himself demanding a lawyer, reciting the classics, and yelling about his Constitutional rights at all hours, that the authorities released him, rather than endure his presence.

A fellow barrister once remarked about English,.

"He may be out-smarted, out-fought, out-thought, and out-maneuvered, but he will never be out-spoken."

In 1887, English was elected by an overwhelming vote to the post of district attorney, a position he held for three full terms.

English was married three times, losing each wife because of his love for whiskey. *John Barleycorn* was a much more important factor in his life than any mere female could ever be. His first wife gave him two sons and his second gave him one. The third lasted only long enough to give him her *opinion* of him!

In 1900, Arizona politics were such that Allen English was assured the offer of the position of United States Commissioner. However, before the offer could be made, English opened his mouth when he should have kept still.

According to old time Arizonians, it always rains on San Juan's Day. When he heard a discussion to that effect in Billy King's Saloon, English's perverse nature made him instantly disagree. He was so convinced that it would not rain that he boasted he would stand naked under the public rain spout if it did. Tradition held on San Juan's Day and it came a downpour. English, true to his word, removed every stitch of clothes and stood naked under the public rain spout.

Some weeks later, a photograph of English under the rain spout with his name below was received in Washington. Not long after, he was denied the post of United States Commissioner.

As the years passed, English slipped more and more into the role and habits of an alcoholic.

When the Cochise County Courthouse was moved from Tombstone to Bisbee, he went along, although he was seldom involved in any legal work at all.

Allen English died penniless and alone on November 8, 1937. His favorite and oft-heard expression still lives on with the ghost of Tombstone:

"Oh moon, thou art full!
But you ain't a damn bit ahead of me!"

At the The Tombstone Courthouse steps
Left to right, standing: *Bill Bradley—Deputy Sheriff; George W. Swain County Attorney; Unknown—Clerk; A.H. Emanuel—Clerk of Court; Unknown; William Richie—Jailer; Nat Hawke.*
Seated center: *D.K. Wardell; Mrs. Bluette.*
Seated lower row: *W.E. Steahle—Attorney; M.D. Scribner—County Treasurer; H.W. Wentworth—County Recorder; W.D. Monmonier.*

Cosmopolitan Hotel, 1882—A. Billike, Proprietor

Miss Nellie Cashman

9

Nellie Cashman
The Angel Of Tombstone

She was a small, slender woman just a shade over five feet. Her eyes and hair were jet black and her skin was like the petals of a white rose. She spoke with a decided Irish lilt, was a devout Catholic, and followed the mining boom towns from Tombstone to Alaska.

This unusual lady was Nellie Cashman, called by many, the "Angel of Tombstone."

John P. Clum, founder of the *Tombstone Epitaph* once wrote of Nellie as:

"...a noble woman whose energetic, courageous, and self-sacrificing life was an inspiration of the frontier for half a century."

Nellie was born in Queenstown, Ireland in 1844. When still a child, she and her widowed mother came to America and settled in Boston.

Upon leaving Boston, they resided in Washington, D.C., for a short period of time. From the nation's capitol, the two women sailed to Panama, rode burros across that country, then took passage on another ship to complete their journey to San Francisco.

While she was still a young lady, Nellie made quite a name for herself in the mining camps scattered through the West; Coeur d' Alene, Virginia City, Pioche, Tombstone and numerous others.

In 1875, she led a party of six men, with fifteen hundred pounds of supplies, into Telegraph Creek up in the frozen reaches of the far North, to the aid of a party of miners stricken with scurvy. Later that same year, she helped raise funds to build St. Joseph's Hospital in Victoria.

Word of new mining camps blossoming throughout Southern Arizona drew her to Tucson in 1879. She opened Delmonico's Restaurant on the south side of Church Plaza. Her cooking was superb and her new business did well.

But then the stories of a new silver strike began to drift in, stories about a camp called Tombstone. Nellie could not ignore the lure of a new boom town, so she sold her restaurant to Mrs. M.J. Smith.

Arriving in Tombstone she took a partner, Jenny Swift, and the two ladies opened a fruit and provision store. The tiny Irish lass also

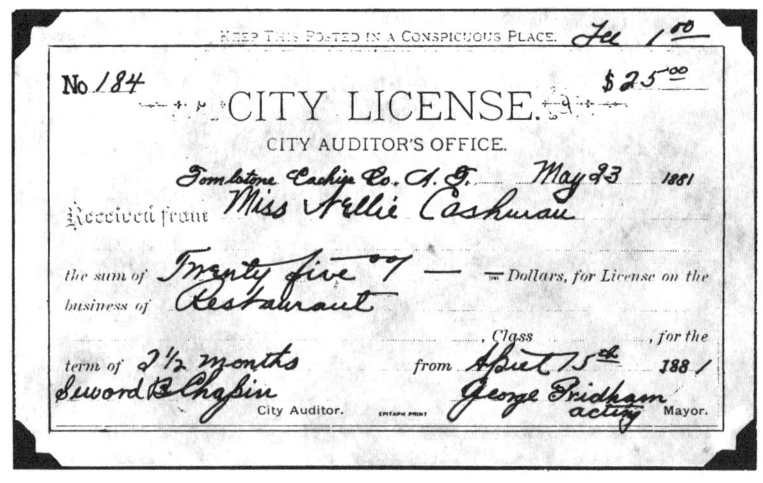

KEEP THIS POSTED IN A CONSPICUOUS PLACE. Fee 1.00

No 184 $25.00

CITY LICENSE.

CITY AUDITOR'S OFFICE.

Tombstone Cochise Co. A. T. May 23 1881

Received from Miss Nellie Cashman

the sum of Twenty five 00/ — Dollars, for License on the business of Restaurant

, Class , for the term of 2½ months from April 15th 1881

Seward B. Chapin City Auditor. EPITAPH PRINT George Pridham acting Mayor.

City License issued to Miss Nellie Cashman May 23, 1881

purchased the Russ House, located at the corner of Fifth and Toughnut Streets, and converted it into a hotel and restaurant. It became known as Nellie Cashman's Hotel and still carries that name today.

When her brother-in-law died, her sister, Frances, and her five children moved into a small home just back of the hotel. The two sisters opened the American Hotel in 1882. Nellie invested wisely and, in time, became the owner of a grocery store and a saloon in addition to her other holdings. She hired a man to run the saloon and would not go near it.

Frances died a few years later and Nellie raised and educated her three nieces and two nephews. Although she made a great deal of money, it always went to help people who were sick or down on their luck. Frequently, her hotel was converted into a free hospital with Nellie serving as a nurse.

Many of her fund-raising drives received large sums of money from the saloons and the *"Red Light District."*

Back in July, 1881, Nellie had brought three Sisters of Mercy to Tombstone to take over the City and County Hospital. Earlier, in 1880, she had assisted the Sisters of St. Joseph in opening St. Mary's Hospital in Tucson. This was the first "non-military" hospital in Arizona.

Nellie was instrumental in building one of the first schools in Tombstone, and Tombstone's first Catholic Church, located at Safford and Sixth Streets.

One Tombstone story relates that, when a drummer staying at the Russ House complained about Nellie's beans, a miner, frequently befriended by Nellie, overheard his remark. The miner walked over and placed a cocked six-gun to the man's head and quietly suggested that he eat every bean on his plate and pretend to enjoy them. The drummer ate with enthusiasm and said no more.

Sam Lee was a Chinese cook employed by Nellie in Tombstone. Nellie gave him a leave of absence to pay a visit to China. As he was departing, he asked her to give him a photograph of her.

"Me tak'em pictue to China, Sam said, "Me get him Chinaman paint fine pictue of you, Missy Cashman, and me fetch'em fine pictue back to you."

Sam got the photo and he had his artist friend in China paint a portrait of his beloved employer.

In 1884, Dan Kelly, Omar Sample, James Howard, Dan Dowd, and Bill Delaney awaited their execution date at the Tombstone Court House for murders they had committed during a hold-up, referred to by locals as the *"Bisbee Massacre."* Sheriff J.L. Ward announced that the execution of these men would take place:

"at the Court House, Tombstone, Arizona on March, 28, 1884, at one o'clock."

As the murders committed by these men had been unprovoked and in cold blood, the interested public wished to watch them meet their end. An enterprising carpenter leased the adjacent vacant lot and built a grandstand overlooking the courtyard. He busily engaged himself in selling tickets to any individuals who wished to view the executions. The doomed men resented such proceedings and their complaints reached Nellie Cashman. She held a meeting with twenty or more of her miner friends and outlined her plan.

At 2:00am on the day of the execution, Nellie and her miners, laden with drills, crowbars, hammers, picks, and sledges made their way to the courthouse. By the time the pink of dawn arrived the grandstand seats had been reduced to splinters and tossed into a nearby dry wash.

Constable, the carpenter who had built the seats, soon discovered that he was unemployed in Tombstone and was becoming genuinely unpopular. Nellie had spread the word that he was an undesirable citizen.

Two of the doomed men were Catholics and Nellie converted the other three. Rumors were rife that their bodies were to be given to medical research for dissection after they had been hanged. She promised that this would not happen and that their graves would not be desecrated.

She saw the five bodies decently interred in Boothill

Fred Dodge
friend of Nelly Cashman and undercover agent of Wells-Fargo

and at dusk that day and on the ten following evenings two old prospectors disappeared into the deepening gloom. They maintained a careful watch on the graves as had been promised by Nellie Cashman. None of the graves were molested. Later that same year, Nellie saved the life of E.B. Gage, Superintendent of the Grand Central Mining Company.

The miners were on strike and in a nasty mood. Their demands were not being met. To expedite matters in their cause, they decided to kidnap and hang E.B. Gage. Somehow, Nellie learned of the striker's plans and, late that same night, she drove a buggy up to Gage's house. Mr. Gage climbed in and the buggy moved slowly through town. The journey continued to Benson, where Gage caught a train for Tucson.

Fred Dodge, a citizen of Tombstone during the 1880's, and an undercover man for Wells-Fargo once wrote of Nellie:

"Nellie Cashman was one of the most wonderful women I ever met. She was unique. Though she seemed to prefer to associate with men, there was never a spot on her moral character. I knew her in Nevada and in California before either of us reached Tombstone. In every place where I knew her she was the queen of the Irish miners, and held the respect of the 'Cousin Jacks' as well. Indeed, this high opinion of her was held by all right-thinking men. She was very out-spoken, and sometimes made ene--mies by her uncensored express-ions of opinion. I have always regarded Nellie as a most remarkable and admirable woman."

Marcus Aurelis Smith
well-known lawyer

In 1883 there was a gold stampede into Lower California.

The new gold strike was supposed to lie in the vicinity of the tiny Mexican village called Muleje on the Gulf of California opposite the city of Guaymas.

A party was formed to journey to the gold strike, totalling less than a dozen men - and Nellie Cashman.

Included in this group were Marcus Aurelius Smith, later to become a United States Senator from the State of Arizona, and Milton E. Joyce, one time owner of the Oriental Saloon and past supervisor of Cochise County and, of course, Nellie, dressed in overalls, flannel shirt, boots and wide-brimmed Stetson.

Milton E. Joyce
Owner of the Oriental
—courtesy Harry Stewart

Arriving in Guaymas, Mexico, they chartered a boat to ferry them across the Gulf. They were deposited in an extremely inhospitable region to begin their search for gold nuggets.

Many days of searching brought them nothing, except the sudden realization that they were out of water!

Nellie was still in much better physical condition than any of the others. She volunteered to go search for water. Strangely enough, in that remote and desolate region, she found an ancient Catholic mission.

Soon, she had several goatskins filled with water and loaded on burros. Without any rest, she immediately rushed back to their camp. She was just in time to save the men, who were badly dehydrated.

With this near-fatal episode, the expedition lost all interest in the search for gold and headed for the seacoast. They waited several days before their ship arrived to take them to Guaymas. Once out to sea they discovered that the ship's captain was roaring drunk. When he threatened their lives they tied him up and put him away below decks. Then they and the crew took the ship into Guaymas.

Once there, they were all arrested and thrown into jail. It seems that the Mexican authorities frowned upon anyone tying up and holding prisoner a ship's captain on the high seas—no matter what the circumstances. They spent several days in a very unsanitary, smelly jail until American Consul Willard managed to have them freed.

Upon receiving their release from jail, the entire group had had enough of Mexico, and were eager to return to Tombstone.

The *Florence Tribune* (Arizona) November 20, 1897, printed the following news item:

"Miss Nellie Cashman, one of the most favorably known women in Arizona, arrived from Yuma yesterday. Miss Nellie is preparing to organize a company for gold mining in Alaska. Her many friends in Arizona will wish her success, for during her twenty years residence in the territory, she has made several fortunes, all of which have gone to charity."

This amazing woman left Tombstone when the mines began to close. She travelled extensively for awhile, even going to Africa, then returned to Arizona to open the Arizona-Silver Belt Restaurant in Prescott in 1898.

When gold was discovered in the Klondike, she took passage on the steamer *"Centennial"* to Skagway. She then went on to Dawson by the Dyea Trail and through White Horse and Five Finger Rapids.

Once in Dawson, she opened the *"Alaskan Delmonico Restaurant."* The price of food was so high that one of her meals cost six dollars. Still, if a man was hungry and broke, she fed him without charge.

After some months, she bought a grocery store in which she set aside an area for reading and writing providing free cigars and tobacco. It was called the *"Prospector's Haven of Rest."*

Nellie Cashman never married, though she had ample opportunity. The miners of every camp admired and respected her. Whenever she entered a saloon, dance hall, or other public building, every man present stood up.

She met many famous people while she was in the North. Among them were Jack London, Jack Crawford, Robert Service, Buck Choquette, Joaquin Miller and a score of others.

Once, she was pleasantly surprised when Wyatt Earp, John Clum and Ed Schieffelin, all old Tombstone friends, dropped in to visit her.

Nellie Cashman
at eighty years

Surely, the lure of the boom towns was a magnet to Nellie Cashman and she always staked a number of mining claims in the hope of striking it rich, not for herself, but to help others. But the real attraction of the mining camps to Nellie was that she could be with the prospectors and miners and function as doctor, nurse, and missionary.

Nellie was a devout Catholic and spent a great part of her time with the Sisters and working for the hospitals.

Nellie stayed seven years in Dawson, leaving there in 1904. When she had disposed of her holdings, she went to Fairbanks and bought a grocery store.

After a few years, she grew tired of that and sold out in 1907. She drove a dog sled five hundred miles to the upper Koyukuk River country where she spent several years prospecting and mining.

At the age of eighty years, she drove a sled and dog team from Koyukuk to Seward, an incredible distance of seven hundred fifty miles over snow and ice in the bitter cold.

During the summer of 1924, Nellie became very ill at her cabin, located at Coldfoot, north of the Arctic Circle. An Episcopal deacon brought her down the Koyukuk River in a small boat. She was taken up the Yukon and Tanana Rivers to St. Joseph's Hospital in Fairbanks.

Doctors found that she had double pneumonia and they could scarcely believe that she had survived that hazardous thousand-mile, journey from Coldfoot. She recovered quickly and was released from the hospital.

Nellie was anxious to get back to her gold claims above the Arctic Circle, but it was soon apparent that she did not have the strength for such a trip.

Friends were finally able to convince her to go "outside" for further medical attention.

Nellie travelled to Victoria, B.C. and entered the Sister's St. Joseph Hospital on October 9, 1924. She was much worse than she had ever admitted. Strength and resistance were nil. She was old and feeble. Nellie knew that she did not have long and she prepared for the end.

She was a revered member of every community in which she had lived or visited, giving generously of mercy, charity, and courage. She was one of the few daring women who braved the rigors and hazards of the boom towns. The *Yukon Midnight Sun,* June 20, 1898, said:

"Miss Cashman is the pioneer woman of this country and is widely known for her good deeds."

Sick and flat broke, this indomitable woman had spent her life helping others. Death took her on January 4, 1925.

Nellie was buried in the Catholic Cemetery at Victoria. For many years her grave had no stone, but the concrete ledge around it carried an inscription:

> ***"NELLIE CASHMAN JANUARY 4, 1925***
> ***80 YEARS BORN IN IRELAND"***

John Clum commented:

"Such an epitaph is insufficient for such an angel."

Grave marker was placed in 1979
by the Sisters of St. Ann

REFERENCES:

1. The Arizona Historical Review, Nellie Cashman, by John P. Clum, January, 1931.
2. Lulu Fairbanks' Collection, University of Alaska, Fairbanks.
3. Tombstone's Immortals, by Ben T. Traywick. Published by Red Marie's Bookstore, 1973.

Virgil Earp

10

Virgil Earp

Marshal of Tombstone

"A bold, daring man with blonde hair, smokey blue eyes, and a sinister expression; he is not a man to trifle with."

This was the 1880 description of Virgil Earp, but it would have described all three of the fighting Earp brothers.

Virgil, the third son of Nicholas Porter Earp, was born in Hartford, Kentucky on July 18, 1843. Not many years later, Nick moved his family into Pella, Iowa, a predominantly Dutch farming community.

Virgil and his brothers grew up tall and strong from the rough, demanding labor of the farm.

In early 1860, at the age of seventeen, Virgil began to keep company with Ellen Rysdam, the fifteen year-old daughter of a Dutch neighbor. The young couple imagined themselves in love and ran off to the adjoining county, where they were married under assumed names.

Nicholas and the old Dutchman were overcome with rage at this untimely and unexpected marriage, and separated the two young people until the union could be annulled.

Since his father and father-in-law would not let him live with his wife, Virgil enlisted in the Union Army, 83rd Illinois Infantry, Company C at Monmouth, on August 21, 1862 to fight in the War Between the States.

All through the war, Virgil believed that Ellen waited for him to return to Pella. Unknown to him, he had been reported killed in action and the story printed in the local newspaper.

He served with the Union forces until the end of the war, participating in three major battles. He was discharged at Nashville, Tennessee on June 26, 1865.

When he had made his long way home to Pella, he was astonished to find that not only was his young wife and her family gone, but his own family as well. The neighbors informed him that Nicholas had taken the Earp family to San Bernadino, California. Further explanation revealed that, after the old Dutchman had convinced Ellen that Virgil was dead, he had taken his entire family up the Oregon Trail to an unknown destination in the Pacific Northwest. Thus, Virgil lost all contact with the girl to whom he had been briefly married.

Virgil turned west, traveling as far as Santa Fe with a wagon train. There he met a group of surveyors and rode with them to the area of Prescott in Arizona Territory. He rode over much of the country around there, liked it immensely, and considered it as a fine place to settle, sometime in the future.

Since he was reasonably close, Virgil decided to pay a visit to his family in California. He arrived in San Bernadino late in December, 1865. The family was overjoyed at his return from the dead and urged him to stay with them.

In the spring of 1866, Virgil found employment as a wagon master for a freight company engaged in hauling goods from California to Prescott. A younger brother, Wyatt, was hired as a teamster. The two brothers worked for this company more than two years.

Nicholas, always prone to move about, decided to move the family to Illinois and Virgil and Wyatt went to work grading for track on the railroad. They stayed until 1869, at which time they collected their wages and rode east to visit the family, presumably well-settled in Illinois. Upon their arrival they discovered that old Nicholas still had the itch to move, as he and the family were now living in Lamar, Missouri. Unperturbed, Virgil and Wyatt rode toward Missouri, where their Uncle Jonathan Earp lived.

Virgil and his father opened a grocery store in Lamar. *'Old Nick'* was also elected Justice of the Peace. While in this capacity, he married his son, Wyatt, to Urilla Sutherland and his son, Virgil, to Rozilla Draggoo.

Author's Note:

"These two marriages are the only evidence the author has ever found concerning the combined six marriages that Virgil and Wyatt supposedly made."

Wyatt also ran for Constable and was elected to office. He was only the second constable Lamar, Missouri had elected.

Virgil did not tarry long in Missouri, but rode out alone— West— working at various jobs along the way.

Author's Note:

"The author has been unable thus far to find any record as to what happened to Rozilla Draggoo."

The year 1873 found Virgil in Council Bluffs, Iowa. That is where he met Alvira Sullivan - "Allie," to him. She was with him for the next 32 years.

Barely five feet tall, Allie was all Irish, the daughter of one John Sullivan. She had been born and raised in Nebraska, not far from Council Bluffs and was a waitress at the hotel where Virgil met her.

Alvira Sullivan Earp
Virgil's wife
—Glenn Boyer collection

Author's Note:

"Allie claimed all her life that she and Virgil were married, but to date no verification has been found."

Evidently, they formed some sort of an alliance, wandering from town to town over the West for the next three years. Feeling a need to settle down somewhere, Virgil recalled Prescott in the Arizona Territory, so they went there.

Virgil and Allie's house at First and Fremont Streets in

Allie and Virgil located a claim not far from Prescott and settled down. Virgil found a part time job carrying the mail, and acted as a deputy for a short while under Sheriff Joseph Walker and again under Sheriff Ed Bowers.

In 1876, two cowboys rode into Prescott and shot up the town. Sheriff Bowers assembled a posse to go out and arrest them. Virgil, a member of the posse, encountered one of them and shot him twice through the heart.

By 1879, the new silver boom town, Tombstone, was beginning to make itself known. Virgil decided to go there, but felt that he needed some sort of job before he departed. With this objective in mind, he talked Marshal Dake into making him a Deputy Marshal in the Tombstone area. Dake appointed him a U.S. Deputy Marshal on November 27, 1879. His commission was filed with the Federal Commissioner's Office in Tucson on that date.

Virgil had written to Wyatt in Dodge City, urging him to come to Tombstone, as there appeared to be unlimited opportunities in the new camp. Wyatt and James left Kansas and Morgan prepared to leave Montana, all headed West to meet Virgil in the new boom town.

Wyatt, Virgil, and Morgan all bore a close resemblance to each other – six feet tall, blonde, and blue-eyed, with long drooping moustaches. People who did not know them well could not tell them apart. All three were well-versed in the use of guns.

Virgil was the best-liked of all the Earp boys, friendly and generous to a fault. Though he and Allie never had children, he loved them and they him.

The news of the discovery of a whole mountain of silver brought thousands of newcomers thronging into Tombstone. Stores, saloons, restaurants, gambling halls, hotels, and dance halls were hurriedly thrown together up and down Allen and Fremont Streets. Allen Street quickly became *"Whiskey Row"* and was a riot of noise and bedlam.

On the night of October 27, 1880, six-guns roared the length of Allen Street. The *"Clanton Gang"* had *"treed"* the town. The gunmen who led the fracas were *"Curly Bill"* Brocius, the McLaury brothers, Frank and Tom; Ike and Billy Clanton, Frank Patterson and Pony Diehl.

FRED WHITE KILLED

Fred White, a fine lawman, had been elected Tombstone's first Marshal ten months previous on January 6, 1880. Now that this wild shooting had been going on for some time, the Marshal knew that he had to disarm the *"Cowboys"* and make an example of them. He sent for Wyatt Earp to assist him.

The two men determined a course of action and agreed that the best plan was for one of them to come from either side to place the drunk *"Cowboys"* between them.

They encountered *"Curly Bill"* just off Allen Street in a vacant lot where the Bird Cage Theatre now stands, with a revolver in his hand.

White ordered him to surrender his weapon and *"Curly Bill"* offered it to him barrel first. The Marshal grasped the gun barrel to take it from the outlaw.

A tongue of flame stabbed through the night followed by the dull roar of a 45. White fell, writhing in agony, shot through the abdomen.

Echoes of the shot had not diminished before Wyatt rapped *"Curly Bill"* several times, rather severely, over the head with his gun barrel. Morgan Earp and Fred Dodge (Wells-Fargo) reached the scene within seconds.

The Earp brothers prowled the streets of Tombstone all night 'till they found every man involved in the shooting of Marshal White except Ike Clanton. Every man they located was pistol-whipped, then dragged off to join *"Curly Bill"* in the local calaboose.

Mayor Randall appointed Virgil Earp as Acting Marshal on October 28, 1880 to finish out White's term. Fred White lived a few days then died. Before his death, he said that *"Curly Bill"* had not purposely shot him, it had been an accident. Accident or not, the shooting of Marshal White by *"Curly Bill"* was the opening incident of the war between the Earps and the *"Cowboy"* faction. More were soon to follow.

In January, 1881, Virgil ran for the office of Town Marshal, but lost the race to Ben Sippy. It was a close race and Virgil lost it because he had made himself unpopular with the rather strict ordinances that he had persuaded the City Council to make and that he rigidly enforced.

In short, these ordinances:

(1) Barred horses from the sidewalks;

(2) Forbade the riding of horses into any store, saloon, gambling house, honkytonk, or dance hall;

(3) Barred possession of firearms in the city limit except by persons in the process of entering or leaving town;

(4) Ordered all persons to check their firearms immediately upon their arrival in town;

(5) Prohibited the discharging of firearms in the town limits except on holidays and the day preceding; and

(6) Provided the Marshal with the authority to arrest anyone that he considered a nuisance.

Ike Clanton

These six ordinances and their enforcement cost Virgil the election. Not long after Ben Sippy assumed office, Michael O'Rourke, known as *"Johnny-Behind-the-Deuce,"* shot and killed Henry Schneider, the Chief Engineer of the Tombstone Mining and Milling Corporation in Charleston. Johnny was arrested and placed in jail.

George McKelvey, the Charleston Constable, saw an angry mob forming and realized that he could not protect his prisoner. He released O'Rourke, placed him in a buckboard pulled by a team of mules and headed for Tombstone. There, O'Rourke was taken to Vogan's Bowling Alley where Morgan Earp guarded him while Wyatt, Virgil, and Ben Sippy faced the angry miners outside.

By June, 1881, the *"Cowboys"* had Marshal Ben Sippy pretty well rattled. It is evident that he considered the job too much to handle and the town too tough for him as he applied for a leave of absence, took it, and disappeared forever.

John Clum was now the Mayor of Tombstone and, when it was apparent that Sippy was gone for good, he called a meeting of the City Council and gave the office to Virgil again.

On July 4, 1881, Virgil became the permanent Chief of Police, Marshal, Health Inspector, and Fire Marshal. His office was located upstairs above the Crystal Palace Saloon. The Earps and the *"Cowboy"* gang had several more minor clashes and the time for violence drew near. *"Curly Bill,"* Ringo, Ike Clanton and the McLaury brothers boasted in the saloons on Allen Street that they intended to run the Earps out of town.

On the morning of October 26, 1881, Virgil received a report that a heavily-armed Ike Clanton was in town and boasting that he had come to kill a few Earps.

Virgil and Morgan began a search for Ike. On Fourth Street, Virgil spotted him as he stepped out of a doorway and went cautiously up the street. Virgil walked quietly up behind Ike and spoke to him. Ike tried to swing his Winchester around to shoot Virgil, but the lawman split his scalp with his pistol. The marshal then dragged Ike down to Justice Wallace's Court where he was fined twenty-five dollars for disturbing the peace.

When the news of these threats were known, the Citizens Safety Committee went to Marshal Virgil Earp and offered to back him up with guns, but Virgil said that it was his job and that he wanted no help except that of his brothers.

As the scene began to unfold, Doc Holliday demanded that he be allowed to accompany them when they confronted the *"Cowboys."* So it was that the Earps and Holliday faced Tom and Frank McLaury, Ike and Billy Clanton, in that vacant lot adjacent to the O.K. Corral.

During that confrontation guns roared and thundered for a brief interval then subsided leaving three men dead and two seriously wounded. This now famous gun battle lasted less than half a minute, yet the controversy arising from it has endured over the years.

The names of the participants have become immortal in Western history and legend. The Earps: Virgil, Wyatt, and Morgan, and Doc Holliday walked down Fremont Street to the O.K. Corral, to their destinies, and into the blood-stained pages of Tombstone history.

Final results of the gunfight were Frank and Tom McLaury and Billy Clanton dead; and Virgil and Morgan wounded. The Marshal was shot through the calf of the right leg, the ball going clear through. His brother, Morgan, was shot through the shoulders, the ball entering the point of the right shoulder blade, following across the back, shattering off a piece of vertebrae and passing out the left shoulder.

Dr. George Emory Goodfellow

The Nugget printed the following statement after the gunfight:

"The 26th of October, 1881, will always be marked as one of the crimson days in the annals of Tombstone, a day when blood flowed as water, and human life was held as a shuttle cock, a day to be remembered as witnessing the bloodiest street fight that has ever occurred in this place, or probably in the Territory."

Not to be outdone the pro-Earp *Epitaph* had this to say:

"The feeling among the best class of our citizens is that the Marshal (Virgil) was entirely justified in his efforts to disarm these men, and that being fired upon they had to defend themselves which they did most bravely."

The bodies of the three dead men were dressed in expensive store clothes, laid out in caskets and placed on exhibit at the *Ritter & Ream Funeral Parlor.*

A sign which read:

"MURDERED IN THE STREETS OF TOMBSTONE"

was placed above the bodies. Regardless of all evidence and opinions to be found, Judge Wells Spicer heard the case and ordered the Earps and Holliday released from all charges.

Retaliation from the *"Cow- boys"* was sure to come.

Near midnight of Wednesday, December 28, 1881, bushwhackers struck from ambush. Virgil had left the Oriental Saloon and started toward the Crystal Palace, crossing Fifth Street, when the flame and roar of shotguns blasted at him from the darkness.

Two of the shots struck Virgil, one badly shattering his left arm, the other entering his left side. The others went through the windows of the Crystal Palace. It was evident that there were three men armed with double-barrel shotguns, as five shots were fired in rapid succession. Nineteen holes from the shots fired at Virgil were found in the outside wall of the saloon.

Dr. Goodfellow removed four inches of shattered bone from Virgil's

Frank Stilwell was killed down tracks (to the right) by Wyatt Earp on March 20, 1881 (two nights following the killing of Morgan Earp by Stilwell in Tombstone). On the left: the S.P.R.R Tucson Depot. The San Xavier Hotel is on right.

left arm and twenty buckshot from his side and back. These wounds were to cripple him for life. The assassins were afraid of Virgil and stationed themselves too far away for the shotguns to be effective in killing him. They had concealed themselves upstairs in the two story building being constructed for the Huachuca Water Company—all the way across Allen Street.

The men responsible for the attack on Virgil were, as to be ex-

pected, Ike and Phin Clanton, Frank Stilwell, Johnny Barnes, John Ringo, Hank Swilling and Pete Spencer.

The Clantons later surrendered to a posse led by Pete Spencer. They were charged with attempted murder, but, due to a technicality, the case was thrown out.

Judge Stillwell dismissed the case against the ambushers, stating that the case was not valid because the warrant had been served by John H. Jackson, who was not a legally constituted officer and had no authority to arrest or hold anyone.

Wyatt realized that Sheriff Behan and the courts were protecting the *"Cowboys"* in every way possible, so he did not pursue the case.

Only a short time had passed, when the assassins struck again on March 18, 1882. This time, their victim was Morgan Earp. He was playing pool with Bob Hatch at Campbell & Hatch's Saloon between Fourth and Fifth Streets on Allen, when a shot fired from the darkness of the alley shattered his spine and snuffed out his life.

A Coroner's Jury determined that Morgan's murderers were Frank Stilwell, Indian Charlie, Pete Spencer, and Joe Doe Freis.

Morgan's body was shipped to Colton, California for burial. Virgil, who was still practically helpless, went along with the body. Accompanying him were Allie and Louisa Earp. Wyatt and Warren Earp,

Sherman McMasters, *"Turkey Creek Jack"* Johnson, *"Texas Jack"* Vermillion and Doc Holliday escorted them to Tucson, as they feared another ambush if Virgil went alone.

U.S. Marshal Crawley Dake had telegraphed to Wyatt his appointment as Deputy Marshal upon receiving the news of Virgil's injuries. This appointment was effective on December 29, 1881.

Frank Stilwell had the misfortune to encounter Wyatt and his friends in the Tucson rail yard as they were seeing Virgil off.

An excerpt from the *Epitaph* tells of the finding of Frank Stilwell's body:

"This morning at daylight, the track man from the Southern Pacific Railroad found the body of Frank Stilwell about 100 yards north of Porter's Hotel at the side of the track, riddled with bullets."

A Tucson Coroner's Jury named Wyatt and Warren Earp, Doc Holliday, *"Texas Jack,"* and McMasters as the men who had killed Stilwell. A judge issued warrants for their arrests.

After the departure of Virgil with Morgan's body, Wyatt, Doc Holliday, and their friends accounted for most of the men who had any part in the ambushing.

When Virgil and Allie reached California, he was still in agony and his health, otherwise, beginning to deteriorate. During the next several months, he consulted a number of specialists in San Francisco and underwent several operations—all of which improved his condition little, if any.

As soon as he had regained strength enough, Virgil and Allie moved to Calico, a new, silver boom town in the desert country of eastern California. In the next few years they kept moving from one mining camp to another in California, Utah, Texas, Nevada, Idaho and Colorado.

Nicholas Earp, now in Colton, California, was elected Justice of the Peace in 1884. Virgil and Allie moved to Colton in 1886, and Virgil ran for the office of Constable. He won the election by one hundred thirty-six votes to one hundred twenty-seven.

Colton was incorporated on July 12, 1887, and Virgil became the town's first marshal, taking office on July 11, 1887. "Old Nick" was appointed city recorder two weeks later.

Virgil refereed the first legal boxing match held in San Bernardino. The match was thirty-two rounds, between Joe Cotton and Jack Sullivan on December 24, 1889.

Defeated in the election of April, 1890, Virgil bought the house at 528 West "H" Street in Colton for Allie. A few months later he purchased a gambling hall on the north side of San Bernardino's Third Street.

A new gold strike in the New York Mountains in April of 1893 created another stampede. This time, Virgil went as a businessman, building the only two-story building in the new town of Vanderbilt. He named this building Earp Hall.

The Vanderbilt gold rush did not last long and was practically over by 1895. Virgil sold Earp Hall and left Vanderbilt that year. During their stay there, Virgil's health showed a marked improvement, and he regained some use of his crippled left arm.

In 1895, Wyatt wrote Virgil and convinced him that they should go into business in Cripple Creek, Colorado. Virgil went but the venture was evidently not successful as he appeared in Prescott in 1896.

Virgil worked at various places, gambling, and a short while at mining in the old Grizzly Mine.

Wyatt always had get-rich schemes and usually involved Virgil. When he heard about the Yukon gold rush, he quickly decided to go and wrote Virgil in an attempt to persuade him to go along.

As usual, Virgil was tempted, but Allie was tired of all the continuous moving and she talked Virgil out of going.

Wyatt went North, but without Virgil. While mining near Prescott, Virgil was seriously injured in a cave-in. Both his feet were crushed and his hip dislocated. Old wounds, accidents, and general ill health were beginning to take their toll.

THE LAST LETTER

In 1899 Virgil received a strange letter. It had been written by a lady in the state of Oregon. She inquired whether he was the Virgil Earp who had once been the Marshal of Tombstone, and if he had known a girl named Ellen, who had lived in Pella, Iowa, before he went to fight in the War Between the States. If so, she believed him to be her father and her name was Jane. She went on to say that her mother had believed for many years that Virgil had been killed in the war. Then Jane and she had read about the Earps and the Gunfight at the O.K. Corral in the newspapers. Jane had written a letter to Virgil then, but he did not get it as he had already left Tombstone.

It was a long while before she wrote again and this last letter had followed Virgil west before it was delivered to him. Because Ellen thought him dead, she had eventually married Thomas Easton of Walla Walla, Washington in 1867.

Virgil was astounded to discover that he had a grown daughter. He immediately wrote and invited her to come for a visit.

Jane came, and Virgil and Allie grew quite fond of her, as they had no children of their own. In turn Jane was extremely happy to have found a father she had long believed dead. She was to visit them several times before Virgil's death. In 1900, news came from Arizona that the youngest Earp brother, Warren, had been killed in a Willcox saloon.

The people of Willcox say that Warren was prone to try to live up to the reputation of his brothers. Still, when Boyett shot him down, Warren had been unarmed except for a pocket knife.

Virgil and Wyatt always maintained that Boyett had been used as a tool to kill Warren for revenge on the older brothers.

Local stories told in Cochise County have always related that Virgil and Wyatt took the long trip to Willcox to investigate Warren's death and that they killed Boyett and the man who hired him to kill Warren.

These accounts are more than likely correct, as both Virgil and Wyatt were known to disappear to places unknown at odd times and railroad travel to Willcox from any point in the west was very convenient.

At any rate, John Boyett disappeared, and no trace has been seen of him again. There is not even any mention of him in newspapers or legal documents, and it is extremely difficult to believe that the Earp boys would allow a brother to be killed for any reason, and not avenge his death.

Shortly after the turn of the century, Wyatt was living in the new boom town of Tonopah, Nevada. He wrote Virgil a letter describing the town and telling him gold was plentiful.

Now Virgil could no more resist the call of a new boom town, than a starving man could food, but before he and Allie could get packed up, an even better strike was made. This new town was Goldfield and they arrived there in 1904.

Virgil had hardly settled in before he was made a deputy sheriff and also hired as a special officer at the National Club.

Tex Rickard hired Wyatt in his Northern Saloon, which was next door to the National Club. In 1905, still in Goldfield, Virgil developed pneumonia.

By spring he seemed to be recovering, but suddenly suffered a relapse. The old wounds he received in Tombstone weakened him, and he was unable to resist the illness. Steadily, he grew worse and died in a short time.

As he and Jane had requested, Allie shipped his body to his daughter in Portland, Oregon.

Jane had him buried in Portland's *Riverview Cemetery.*

REFERENCES:

1. Nicholas Porter Earp's family record in a letter to Ben T. Traywick, Reba Earp Young; Lamar, Missouri, dated February 6, 1986. (Copy in Traywick collection).

2. *I Married Wyatt Earp,* by Glenn Boyer, University of Arizona Press, 1976.

3. Illinois State Historical Society Library.

4. Regimental Muster-Out Roll dated June 26, 1865. (Copy in Traywick collection).

5. Virgil's marriage to Rozilla Draggoo. Recorded May 30, 1870, L.N. Timmons, Clerk. (Copy in Traywick collection).

6. Appointment as Deputy Sheriff for Yavapai County December 12, 1877, signed by Ed Bowers. (Copy in Traywick collection).

7. Bond for Office of Constable; Signed by V.W. Earp, Woodworth Thompkins, and A.J. Mason in the amount $1,000.00, dated December 2, 1878. Oath of Office for Virgil Earp, Constable, Territory of Arizona, County of Yavapah, dated December 4, 1878, Win. Wilkensen, Clerk District Court, 3rd Judicial District. (Copies in Traywick collection).

8. Virgil Earp's Oath of Office, U.S. Deputy Marshal, Territory of Arizona, Tucson, dated November 27, 1879, signed by the District Clerk. (Copy in Traywick collection).

9. Bond, Chief of Police V.W. Earp to the Mayor and Common Council of the city of Tombstone, July 5, 1881. (Copy in Traywick collection).

10. *Tombstone Nugget,* January 27, 1882.

11. *Tucson Daily Star,* February 4, 1882.

"Big Nose" Kate Horony

—Glenn Boyer collection

11

"Big Nose" Kate

Much of the history concerning *"Big Nose Kate"* Horony, (Fisher, Melvin, Elder, Holliday, Cummings) of Tombstone fame, was a very elusive mystery until just a few years ago when Earp researcher, Glenn Boyer, unraveled the tangled web of her life.

Boyer discovered that Kate was actually born in Budapest, Hungary on November 7, 1850. Her parents, Michael and Katharina, christened her Mary Katherine Horony.

In 1863, the Horony family moved to Davenport, Iowa. Both parents died a short time later. The children were placed under a guardianship.

Kate ran away in 1867, by stowing away on a steamboat heading south. For awhile, she assumed the name of Kate Fisher. Little is known of her until she appeared in Wichita in 1874 as Kate Elder. The next year, she was working in a dance hall in Dodge City.

In Ft. Griffin, Texas, in the fall of 1877, Kate met the only important man in her life: Doc Holliday.

Doc was dealing cards in John Shanssey's Saloon when they met. Holliday was a well-educated Southern gentleman. Kate was a frontier dance hall woman and prostitute. An unlikely alliance, true, but one that endured—on and off—all Doc's life.

It was quite true that Kate's nose was *"prominent,"* but her other features were *quite* attractive. Her more-than-ample curves were generous and all in the right places.

Tough, stubborn, fearless, and high-tempered, she worked at the business of being a madam and a prostitute because she liked it. She belonged to no man or no madam's house, but plied her trade as an individual in the manner she chose.

Holliday had already earned the reputation of being a cold-blooded killer. Many believed that he liked to kill, but it was not true at that time. He was simply a hot-tempered Southerner who stood aside for no man.

Bat Masterson once remarked,

"Doc Holliday was afraid of nothing on earth."

Doc could be described as a fatalist. He knew that he was condemned to a slow, painful death. If his death should come about quick and painless, who was he to object. Actually, he always expected a quick demise because of the violent life he led, and was visibly disappointed when it did not occur.

John Henry "Doc" Holliday

A Fort Griffin tough guy named Ed Bailey, sat in a poker game with Doc Holliday. Bailey had become accustomed to having his way, with *no* one questioning his actions. Doc's reputation seemed to make no impression on him whatever. In a very obvious attempt to irritate Doc, Bailey kept picking up the discards and looking through them. This was strictly against the rules of western poker, and anyone who broke this rule forfeited the pot. Holliday warned Bailey twice, but the would-be badman ignored the protests. The very next hand, Bailey picked up the discards again. Without a word, Doc raked in the pot, not showing his hand. Bailey brought out a pistol from under the table but, apparently, Doc expected such action, for a large knife seemed to just *"appear"* in his hand.

Then, before the local bully could pull the trigger, Doc, with one slash, completely disemboweled him. Spilling blood every where, Bailey sprawled across the table.

Doc believed it was obvious that he was only protecting himself and in the right, so he stuck around and allowed the marshal to arrest him. That quickly turned into a mistake as, once he had been disarmed and locked up, Bailey's friends and the town's vigilantes began a clamor for his blood.

"Big Nose" Kate knew that Doc was finished, unless someone did something and quick! Likely as not, the local lawmen would turn him over to the mob. Kate took action by setting fire to an old shed. It burned so rapidly that the flames threatened to engulf the entire town. Everyone went to the fire with the exception of three people: Kate, Doc, and the officer who guarded him.

As soon as the lawman and his prisoner were alone, Kate stepped in and confronted them. Kate grasped a pistol in each hand. Disarming the startled guard, Kate passed a weapon to Doc and the two of them vanished into the night.

All that night, they hid in the brush, carefully avoiding parties of searchers. The next morning, they headed for Dodge City, four hundred miles away, on *"borrowed"* horses.

When they arrived in Dodge, the couple registered at Deacon Cox's Boarding House as Dr. and Mrs. J.H. Holliday. Doc felt he owed Kate a great deal for rescuing him from a hang-tree in Ft. Griffin and was determined to do everything he could to make her happy. Kate gave up being a prostitute and inhabiting the saloons. Doc gave up gambling and hung out his shingle again. This was in December, 1877. Apparently Doc had good intentions, as the local paper carried the following ad:

"J.H. Holliday, Dentist, very respectfully offers his professional services to the citizens of Dodge City and surrounding country during the summer. Office at Room No. 24, Dodge House. Where satisfaction is not given, money will be refunded."

However, all his good intentions went for nothing, as they were totally unappreciated. Kate stood the quiet and boredom of respectable living as long as she could. Then she told Doc that she was going back to the bright lights and the excitement of the dance halls and gambling dens. Consequently, the two split up, as they were destined to do many times during the remainder of Doc's life.

September, 1878 found Doc back dealing faro in the Long Branch Saloon. He and Kate spent part of their time together, usually until a violent quarrel sent one of them off. During one of their peaceful times, they left Dodge and went to Trinidad, Colorado.

Shortly after they arrived in town, a young gambler, known as *"Kid Colton"* picked a fight with Doc. Doc's gun roared twice and Colton collapsed in the dust of the street, seriously wounded. Under such circumstances, Doc did not wish to linger around, and rode on to Las Vegas, New Mexico, arriving there about Christmas, 1878.

In the summer of 1879, Doc tried his hand as a dentist for the last time in Las Vegas. He opened his dental office in the same building that William Leonard had a jewelry store. Friendship with Leonard was destined to bring him problems at a later date.

Doc's comeback as a dentist was a weak attempt. Kate's quarrelsome attitude did not help matters, and Doc gambled too much. Thus, the attempt ended in a short time and Doc bought a saloon on Centre Street.

In October, 1879, Wyatt Earp and Mattie along with Jim Earp and Bessie, arrived in Las Vegas enroute to Prescott, Arizona. They invited Doc and Kate to come along with them. Virgil and Allie Earp were already in Prescott, having been there since July, 1877. Morgan Earp was on his way from Montana.

The Earps went on to Tombstone from Prescott without Holliday, who was having a fantastic run of luck at the poker tables. He and Kate reached Tombstone in the summer of 1880, Doc with forty thousand dollars of the Prescott gambler's money in his pockets.

In Tombstone, Doc found Kate living quarters sandwiched between a funeral parlor and the Soma Winery on the north side of Allen Street at Sixth Street. Once they were settled in town, Holliday and *"Big Nose"* Kate took up where they had left off. Although they lived together, Doc went back to drinking and gambling and Kate to her operations as a prostitute and madam.

Joe and *"Rowdy Kate"* Lowe (common law attachment) had arrived in Tombstone about the same time that *"Big Nose"* Kate did. They had known each other back in Dodge City. Now they decided to go into business. They purchased a large tent, rounded up several girls, and a few barrels of cheap whiskey and opened Tombstone's first sporting house. Doc and Kate's arguments were frequent, but not really serious until Kate got drunk and abusive. Doc, at this point, decided that enough was enough and threw her out.

As fate would have it, four masked men attempted to hold up the stage near Contention on March 15, 1881. In this attempt they killed two men: Eli *"Budd"* Philpot, the stage driver, and Peter Roerig, a passenger.

The *"Cowboy"* faction immediately seized upon this opportunity and accused Holliday of being one of the hold-up men. When Bill Leonard, the Las Vegas jeweler and friend of Doc's, was found to be one of the killers, it appeared to be even more logical.

At the same time, Kate was on one of her drunken binges, still berating Doc for throwing her out. While she was airing her troubles with Doc in public, Sheriff Behan and County Supervisor, Milt Joyce, found her and bought her all the whiskey she wanted. They sympathized with her and persuaded her to sign an affidavit that Doc had been one of the masked highwaymen that had killed *"Budd"* Philpot.

On July 5, 1881, a warrant was issued by Justice Spicer for the arrest of Doc Holliday, charging him with complicity in the murder of *"Budd"* Philpot, and the attempted stage robbery near Contention. He was arrested by Sheriff Behan. The warrant had been issued upon the affidavit of Kate Elder. Judge Spicer released Holliday on five thousand dollars bail.

On July 10, 1881, the case against Doc was called for hearing. The district attorney said that he had examined all of the witnesses and that he was satisfied that there was not the slightest evidence to show guilt of the defendant, that the witnesses' statements did not even provide a suspicion of the guilt of the defendant. Then upon his request, the court dismissed.

Once this was over, Kate sobered up and said she signed a paper while drinking with Behan and Joyce, but she could not remember what it was. Then she found she was charged with two drunk and disorderlies that cost her twelve dollars and fifty cents.

Kate was also charged with "threats against life" and faced the U.S. Court on a writ of habeas corpus, presented by her attorney, Judge Wells Spicer. She was brought before T.J. Drum, Court Commissioner of the First Judicial District, who, after due deliberation, ordered the defendant discharged and the writ dismissed.

A short time later, Kate went back to Globe. Most likely she worked in a hotel restaurant while there, possibly for the next three years. She did visit Doc in Tombstone on occasion, but only a few days each time.

Her last visit there was when the Gunfight at O.K. Corral occurred. Kate was in Doc's room at Fly's Boarding House the morning of October 26, 1881, when Ike Clanton came looking for Doc with a rifle. She saw the gunfight through the window of Doc's room. A few days later she went back to Globe.

Kate was apparently in Colorado from 1882 until sometime in 1888, although there is, at present, no evidence that she was with Doc at any time during that period. He went to Glenwood Springs in the Spring of 1887 and died there in November that year.

Kate married a blacksmith, named George M. Cummings, in 1888. They moved to Bisbee, Arizona (24 miles from Tombstone) in 1895.

The Cochise Hotel, Cochise, Arizona where "Big Nose" Kate was employed around the turn of the century.

In 1897, they moved over to the Pearce District. Cummings worked for the mines and Kate did the cooking for the miners.

Her husband was a hard drinker and spent his money for little else. In 1899, Kate left him and moved to the tiny railroad town of Cochise.

Author's Note:

"Cummings committed suicide in Courtland, Arizona on July 7, 1915. A Coroner's Jury said that he killed himself because he had an incurable cancer of the head."

Cochise had been born in 1886 as a railroad station and post office at the junction of the Arizona Eastern and the Southern Pacific railroads. John J. Rath hired Kate to work in his Cochise Hotel in 1899, although the customers never knew her true identity.

The hotel closed in 1900 and Kate became a housekeeper for John J. Howard in the mining town of Dos Cabezas in June of 1900. She stayed there for twenty-nine years and six months until Howard's death in 1930.

Howard left Kate a few acres of property and five mining claims, none of it worth much.

In 1931, she wrote to the Governor of Arizona, George W.P. Hunt, requesting admission to the *"Arizona Pioneer's Home."* Actually, she was not eligible, being foreign born, but she claimed that she had been born in Davenport, Iowa. Governor Hunt gave her permission for admission to the home and she stayed there until her death on November 2, 1940. In five more days she would have been ninety years old.

She is buried in the *Pioneer Cemetery* under the name *Mary K. Cummings.*

REFERENCES:

1. Arizona and the West, O.K. Corral Fight Footnote by Kate Elder, by Glenn Boyer, Spring 1977.

2. *Dodge City Times,* June 8, 1878. (Copy in Traywick collection).

3. *Dodge City Globe,* September 9, 1879 stated: "Mr. Wyatt Earp, who has been on our police force for several months, resigned his position last week and departed for Las Vegas, New Mexico." (Copy in Traywick collection).

4. Census of Inhabitants in Prescott, Yavapai County, June 3, 1880. (Copy in Traywick collection).

5. *Tombstone Daily Nugget,* July, 6, 1881.

6. *Tombstone Daily Nugget,* July 6, 1881.

7. *Tombstone Daily Nugget,* July 10,]881.

8. *Tombstone Daily Nugget,* July 7, 188].

9. *Tombstone Daily Nugget,* July 9, 1881.

10. Coroner's jury report on the death of George M. Cummings, Courtland, Arizona, July, 1915. (Copy in Traywick collection).

Joe Bignon
The Showman of Tombstone

The Bird Cage Theatre

The show must go on in the Bird Cage Theatre Tombstone, Arizona

"Big Minnie" Bignon
"230 lbs of loveliness in pink tights"
(according to Joe)

12

Joe & "Big Minnie" Bignon

When Ed Schieffelin wandered into the Apache-infested desert and discovered a whole mountain of silver, the news spread quickly and the silver camp of Tombstone mushroomed into existence.

Solon M. Allis laid out the townsite on March 5, 1879. One year later Tombstone had a population of one thousand. By June of 1880, there were around three thousand and by 1882, a total of five thousand three hundred people populated this rising boom town.

When Allis had completed the town's lay-out, the lot where the Bird Cage Theatre was later built, was on the Gilded Age mining claim. It was thirty feet by one hundred twenty feet and identified as Lot 9, Block 5 on the south side of Allen Street.

This particular city lot was patented by Mayor Aldar Randall, and Councilmen A.T. Cadwell, Smith Gray, H.H. Jones, and S.B. Comstock on September 22, 1880.

J.S. Clark, M. Gray, J.D. Rouse, and M.E. Clark bought the property on November 8, 1880. It passed through the hands of several owners until Henry Fry and Jerome Ackerson acquired it. Fry lived on the lot until they sold it to William *"Billy"* Hutchinson for the sum of six hundred dollars on July 28, 1881.

Upon acquiring the property, Billy immediately began building the Bird Cage Theatre. Construction was completed late in December, 1881.

At that time the theatre was described as follows:

"The building has one-and-a-half stories, two main rooms, a saloon and a theatre section. Balconies, divided into boxes, run down the length of both sides. Percentage girls distributed drinks to these suspended boxes singing as they served, hence the name Bird Cage. Stage lighting is accomplished by a gas system. Scenery and the backdrops are built and painted by the actors as they need them."

Though the Bird Cage was not the first theater in Tombstone, it was the most popular of its kind. The entertainment it offered consisted of stunts, songs, and dances.

Through the years, the Bird Cage was to be known by a number of names: The Bird Cage Variety Theatre; the Bird Cage Opera House; the Bird Cage; the Elite; and the Olympic.

Billy and Lottie Hutchinson formally opened the Bird Cage on December 26, 1881. First night admission was fifty cents and the audience was entertained with plays, songs, and dances.

Although the Bird Cage attempted valiantly to become respectable, it never did. What the Hutchinsons really wanted was to make the theatre an entertainment spot for Tombstone's respectable families. To do this, they began a "ladies night" whereby all ladies would be admitted free.

Unfortunately, the Bird Cage did not appeal to Tombstone's ladies, as not a single one of them appeared. To be truthful, no proper lady ever entered the Bird Cage during those years. Eventually, it became a mecca for the miners, cowboys, and the *"Ladies of the Night."* It became a notorious establishment where beauty and honor were bought and sold.

In 1882, the *New York Times* wrote that it was the most disreputable bawdy house between Basin Street and the Barbary Coast. It was true that the acts and the audience were equally roguish and the girls-in-waiting, you wouldn't take home to meet mother.

However, the Bird Cage was the inspiration for the song,

"She Was Only A Bird In A Gilded Cage."

The Bird Cage did not close for any reason, but ran continuously, from its opening night of December 23, 1881, until July 2, 1883, at which time the Hutchinsons sold it to Hugh McCrum and John Stroufe.

Joe and Minnie Bignon bought it on January 16, 1886. The Bignons were truly variety show veterans.

Joe Bignon, 1880

Joe Bignon had, even as a child, expressed an intense desire to be an actor. To fulfill this burning ambition, he ran away from home at the tender age of twelve to become a member of Pendergast, Miller, and Kingsley's Minstrels. Later on, he was one of the famous Grant Brothers.

From a young age, Joe had been a variety show minstrel and circus performer. Known throughout Arizona as the *"irrepressible showman,"* Bignon had played Tombstone as early as August, 1879 as a member of the comedy team of Brewster, Skirrow, and Bignon with Brewster's Minstrels.

When he was only twenty, Joe became the proprietor of Miller's Hall in Chicago. The next year he opened Bignon's Varieties in the town of Luddinton, Michigan. In addition to these activities, he also managed another theatre in Anestee, Michigan.

When he joined the Australian Circus, he sold his other interests.

It was his restless nature, all his life, to sacifice everything he had when he wanted to move on to other things.

As the years wore on, he kept moving, from the Australian Circus to Doc Hager's Great Paris Circus then into a partnership with Lou Mudge in a Shebogan, Wisconsin theatre.

In 1879, he dropped everything again and went west to Arizona Territory.

In Tucson, he opened the Park Theatre and in the new silver boom town of Tombstone, the Theatre Comique. While at the Park Theatre, Joe became quite well known for his fine exhibitions of clog dancing. He also received wide acclaim for his famous *"Hottentot"* act in which he performed a comedy dance in a black face monkey suit. The suit had a hook cleverly hidden in the tail. At the climax of his act, he put this hook on a wire stretched between two prop palm trees and swung out over the audience.

Once when he was doing this act, the hook broke during his swing and deposited him into the lap of a member of the audience. Bignon leaped to his feet, and monkey-like scratched his head and under his arm, then bounded onto the stage and disappeared behind the curtains.

Joe went to the Golden Gate City for a visit in 1883, and was offered and accepted the position of manager at the Theatre Comique located at Pine and Kearney Streets. It was unusual for Bignon, but he stayed with this job for two years.

When he left San Francisco, he joined "Harry Leavitts' Combination." This show travelled all through the towns of California and Nevada, giving performances at almost every one of them. When the troupe passed through San Francisco again, Joe quit to join Cushing's Ocean-to-Ocean Circus.

Joe and his wife, *"Big Minnie,"* returned to Tombstone, repainted, redecorated and installed new seats in the Bird Cage, then reopened it as the Elite Theatre. Joe's first show was Frushe's Oriental Circus, whose winter quarters were in Tombstone.

Following that, he changed the theatre's program twice a week, obtaining the majority of his show people from San Francisco. On July 27, 1886, shadowgraphs were shown for the first time.

It was Bignon who organized a stock company to present dramatic performances. Three of the most notable of these were *"One Night in a Barroom," "The Irish Nightingale,"* and *"The Chinese Must Go."*

Through the late 1800's, Joe provided his customers with song and dance numbers, comedians, quick change artists, magicians, and India rubber men.

One of the entertainers hired by Bignon was Professor Ricardo, billed as *"The Wonder of Wonders in Feats of Legerdemain and Hindoo Juggling, Light and Heavy Balancing, Sword Swallowing, Fire-eating, etc."* The Professor was a great attraction, but a few days passed and one evening, while a spellbound audience watched, the Professor was arrested by the county sheriff as an Army deserter from Fort Huachuca.

Other featured attractions were the Ulm Sisters; Will and Frank Heeley, the high kickers and grotesque actors; John Crawford and his *"Fun in a Parlor,"* trick tumbling and contortions and his clown; Ada Prescott, Blanche Leslie, Ella Gardner, and Josie Wilson sang the new songs of that day, and Charley Keene played a black-face comedian and bartender.

In 1887, Bignon decided to go to Kingston, New Mexico and open a variety show. It was not received very well, as he returned to Tombstone after a few months. By now, he had the idea of opening a theatre in every major town in Arizona Territory. As the start of this project he bought an old theatre in Phoenix.

After much effort put forth on the old building and a new show, Joe opened up. However, the venture was a complete disaster as his opening coincided with that of the fair.

For professional purposes, Joe claimed that he was born in Paris and had been specifically trained there for the theatrical profession. The claim was also made that his gifted wife, who was six feet tall and weighed 230 pounds, was a product of London. She was a singer, pianist, and a ballet dancer and sometime prostitute.

Actually Joe was a native of Canada and she a citizen of the United States. *"Big Minnie,"* as she was called, often performed in the Bird Cage. When she was a performer, Joe billed her as:

"Big Minnie: Six feet tall and 230 pounds of loveliness in pink tights."

She frequently filled in as their bouncer too! A story was carried by the Prospector in 1889 concerning a Mexican woodcutter, who violently disagreed with Bird Cage bartender, Charley Keene, over the price of whiskey. Keene asked *"Big Minnie"* to go get Bob Hatch, the marshal, to put the bad man out.

She replied, "You don't need Bob Hatch. I'll put him out myself!" and promptly did so!

The year 1890 saw the decline of drama in the Bird Cage. Joe refused to believe that the interest of the public was waning and organized wrestling tournaments, featuring Cornish wrestlers and weight lifters. In addition he introduced a walking contest. John Forseck and John McCarvin agreed to walk on a track inside the Bird Cage while another show was on, thus giving the customers two shows at once. The walkers had a side bet of fifty dollars. Hoping to once again attract customers, Joe remodeled the Bird Cage and changed its name to the Olympic. He prepared a show of acrobatic feats and dances by the Earl Family Combination. It was unsuccessful.

Bignon gave the same show at Schieffelin Hall, but few people came. By this time, unsuccessful shows had somewhat flattened Joe's pocketbook. In desperation, he sold his theatre in Phoenix for the paltry sum of one hundred dollars. He still had his beloved Bird Cage but it was becoming exceedingly expensive to operate.

Finally Joe gave in, closed the doors in July 1892, and shipped his props to Albuquerque. Evidently, he couldn't forget Tombstone, as in less than half a year, he was back.

There was definitely no demand for variety shows in Tombstone, but Joe was pretty stubborn. This time he opened up shop in the Crystal Palace Saloon. He met with no success this time either and after two years left Tombstone again.

When gold was discovered at Pearce, Joe and *"Big Minnie"* went there. Many of their old friends from Tombstone were already in the new gold camp.

At first, Joe dabbled in real estate, but both he and *"Big Minnie"* yearned for a return to show business. They took two partners, *"Jack the Ripper"* (later killed in the Wildcat Saloon in Benson) and his girl friend, Fern.

Pooling their cash, they built a new fancy saloon called Joe Bignon's Palace. For awhile business was excellent—until John Brockman bought the mine. As the new owner was religious, he set about cleaning up his town. Since the entire town depended solely upon his mine, he had his way.

Business slowly declined until Joe closed his saloon. In 1915 he converted the Palace into a variety theatre called the Idle Hour and later into a moving picture theatre.

The last few years before his death he fell upon hard times. Just before he died, he was operating a soft drink stand near the Pearce Post Office.

Joe Bignon died at the age of eighty-five on December 6, 1925 in Pearce, Arizona, where he had lived for twenty-five years after leaving Tombstone.

"Big Minnie" had passed on in 1900, with Joe following in 1925. Now both lie in eternal rest in the Pearce Cemetery—near their boom town trek.

REFERENCES:

1. *The Arizona Star,* August 18, 1882.
2. *The Arizona Star,* October 22, 1882.
3. Cochise County Records, Book 5, Page 520.
4. *Tombstone Epitaph,* November 13, 1880.
5. *Daily Tombstone Epitaph,* March 7, 1886.
6. *The Arizona Star,* November 14, 1882.
7. *Bisbee Review,* December 8, 1925.
8. *Tombstone Epitaph,* December 11, 1925.

Charleston, Arizona Territory

13

William Claibourne
Arizona's "Billy The Kid"

When John Slaughter drove his cattle from the Texas Panhandle into Tombstone country, a young cowboy by the name of William Claibourne rode along with him. In fact, many of the men who later caused trouble in Tombstone, came to the area with John Slaughter's herds.

Billy was just a good-natured, hard-working, run-of-the-mill cowboy when he first arrived in the San Pedro Valley. However, that wild town of Charleston was close to Slaughter's Ranch and the saloons and the inhabitants there were to be his downfall.

It was while drinking and gambling in these Charleston saloons that he met Johnny Ringo, *"Curly Bill"* Brocius, the Clantons and the McLaurys. All were involved in cattle rustling and highway robbery.

In a jesting manner, the badmen began to call young Claibourne *"Billy the Kid."* Once he had been given the same name as the young New Mexican killer, he began to try to live up to the reputation of the real *"Billy the Kid."*

He was prone to brag that he would make the New Mexican desperado look like a piker.

Claibourne began his reputation by shooting a man named Hickey in Charleston. On October 1, 1881, James Hickey was drunk and in a mean mood. The intended victim of his black mood was nineteen year-old William Claibourne.

Billy left Ben Wood's Saloon to avoid the badgering of Hickey and crossed the street to J.B. Ayer's Saloon. Hickey followed, still taunting the young man. Billy left Ayer's, still trying to avoid Hickey, and headed toward Harry Queen's Saloon.

As he opened the front door of Queen's, Hickey stopped him. Exasperated and his patience at an end, Claibourne turned, pistol in hand, and fired. A blue hole appeared between Hickey's eyes and he slumped to the board sidewalk.

Charleston's Constable, *"Jawbone"* Clark arrested Claibourne, who stood trial in Tombstone, but was acquitted because of Hickeys continued harassment. Thereafter, he was accepted as a badman

Trees to the left of railroad are site of Clanton Ranch

—Glenn Boyer Photo

and known as quick-on-the-trigger. Just days later Claibourne was with his friends, the Clantons and the McLaurys, when their confrontation erupted into a bloody gun battle, leaving the McLaury brothers and Billy Clanton dead and two of the Earps wounded. At that time

Billy showed uncommon good sense by declaring that he was no part of that confrontation and vacating the premises. It could be that he sensed impending doom.

Billy was still around Tombstone when the Earps and Doc Holliday rode out for the last time. A few months later, Johnny Ringo, a friend of Billy's was killed under unusual circumstances and he was extremely upset at this turn of events.

Somehow, he became obsessed with the idea that *"Buckskin Frank"* Leslie had murdered Ringo.

Claibourne went to Globe and took a job working two shifts a day in the smelter. He mentioned that he intended to return to Tombstone and kill Frank Leslie. A number of his friends tried to dissuade him by pointing out that Leslie was a killer, a good shot, and the fastest gun left in Tombstone. Several dead men testified as to his ability with a six-gun. Claibourne would not listen.

On November 14, 1882, Billy Claibourne rode into Tombstone and made his way to the Oriental where Leslie worked as a bartender. Before going to the Oriental, Billy had consumed a large amount of whiskey.

That was his first mistake. Going to the Oriental to accost Frank Leslie was his second and last.Leslie was talking to several men at the bar when Billy entered. He shoved rudely through the men, but Leslie saw that he was drunk and ignored him.

However, when Claibourne began to insult him with profanity, he growled, "Shut up, Billy. You drink too much and you talk too much."

As Billy continued the profanity, Leslie put him out of the saloon and none too gently.

"That's all right, Leslie. I'll get even with you!" Claibourne promised.

"You can see me anytime!" Leslie retorted.

Billy went down Allen Street swearing that he would come back and get even. About an hour later, a man came into the Oriental and informed Frank that Claibourne was outside the door with a Winchester, bragging that he would kill Leslie on sight. Several men had tried to talk him out of it, but he was adamant. Leslie went to the back of the Oriental and out through the double door to Fifth Street.

When he was within shooting distance, he leveled his pistol and called, "Come out, Billy, I don't want to kill you!"

Billy whirled and fired. Frank's pistol roared at almost the same instant. The rifle bullet whistled by Leslie; the pistol bullet struck Billy in the side, inflicting a fatal wound.

The *Epitaph* account of the incident, read:

"BILLY THE KID TAKES SHOT AT BUCKSKIN FRANK THE LATTER PROMPTLY REPLIED AND THE FORMER QUICKLY TURNS UP HIS TOES TO THE DAISIES

Tuesday morning about seven o'clock another tragedy was added to the already long list that have dotted with crimson the history of our city. The causes which led to the affray, so far as they are known, are fully detailed in the coroner's inquest. The survivor of the affair, Frank Leslie, or 'Buckskin' is well known through out the county. William Claibourne, alias 'the Kid'; who precipitated the affair which led to his sudden and untimely taking off, has in the past gained considerable notoriety by his connection with desperate characters and participation in deeds of violence. He was arrested something over a year ago for the murder of Hicks (Hickey) at Charleston, but upon being tried was acquitted. Whatever may have been his record in the past, there is no doubt that at the time he met his death he was engaged in an attempt at assassination, which was frustrated by the coolness and determination of his intended victim. Below we give the statement of Mr. Leslie concerning the unfortunate affair, which is fully corroborated by the coroner's jury."

"Frank Leslie testified: I was talking with some friends in the Oriental Saloon when Claibourne pushed his way among us and began using very insulting language. I took him to one side and said, 'Billy don't interfere. These people are friends among themselves and are not talking politics at all, and don't want you about.'"

"He appeared quite put out and used rather bad and certainly nasty language toward me. I told him there was no use in him fighting with me, that there was no occasion for it and leaving him, I joined my friends. He came back again and began using exceedingly offensive language. I took him by the collar and the coat and led him away, telling him not to get mad. It was for his own good and that if he acted in that manner he was likely to get into trouble. He pushed away from me, using very hard

language, shook a finger at me and said, 'That's all right, Leslie, I'll get even with you', and went out of the Oriental. In a little while a man came in and said there was a man waiting outside to shoot me, but I didn't pay much attention to it. A few minutes later another man came in looking quite white, and said Claibourne was waiting outside with a rifle."

"I then went out and as I stepped from the sidewalk saw about a foot of rifle barrel protruding from the end of the fruit stand. I stepped out in the street and saw that it was Claibourne and said, 'Billy, don't shoot. I don't want you to kill me nor do I want to have to shoot you!'"

Grave marker
Arizona's "Billy The Kid"

"Almost before I finished he raised his gun and shot, and I returned the shot from my pistol, aiming at his breast. As soon as I shot I saw him double up and had my pistol cocked and aimed at him again, when I saw or thought I saw, another man by him, putting his arms around him, and lowered the pistol so that when it discharged the bullet went in the sidewalk. After I fired, I advanced upon him but did not shoot, when he said, 'Don't shoot again, I am killed,' which I didn't, but watched him with my pistol at full cock, as I didn't know what game he might play to get me off my guard. At that time Officer Coyle came up and took hold of my pistol hand. I told him to be careful as it was at full cock. I then uncocked it and gave it to

him and said I would go with him. I told him I was sorry, that I might have done more but I couldn't do less. He then put me under arrest."

"Dr. G.C. Willis, being first duly sworn, said, 'I reside in Tombstone, physician and surgeon by occupa-tion. I saw Mr. Claibourne this morning a little before eight o'clock at my office, being brought there by his friends in a con-dition of shock bordering on collapse. I cut open his shirt and found a gunshot wound in the left side, and an opening in the back next to his spinal column, probably the wound of exit. He was not bleeding very much. I gave him stimu-lants.
I dressed the wound. Then he talked about his opponent and called him a 'murdering son of a b---. Having no convenience there, I sent him to the hospital. In my opinion, it was a fatal wound. He was not dead when he left my office. He said, 'He (Leslie) was a murdering son of a b---, to shoot a man in the back.' I was examining the back when he made that remark. I think he received the wound in the front."

"The coroner's jury listened to the testimony of a number of witnesses, then speedily reached a decision. William Claibourne was killed by a pistol bullet wound inflicted by Frank Leslie, who shot in self-defense and was justified in doing so."

"Billy the Kid" Claibourne's only claim to fame is the fact that he lies in Tombstone's Boothill, not far from the grave of James Hickey, listed as "Buckskin Frank" Leslie's second victim in...
"The town too tough to die."

REFERENCES:

1. *Tombstone Epitaph,* November 18, 1882.

2. Coroner's Inquest of the body of William Claibourne at Tombstone, Arizona, November 14, 1882.

3. The Residents of Tombstone's Boothill, by Ben T. Traywick. Red Marie's Bookstore, 1971.

4. Tombstone's "Buckskin Frank", by Ben T. Traywick. Red Marie's Bookstore, 1985.

Officer Kiv Phillips

14

Filemeno Orante

Cold-Blooded Murderer

Filemeno Orante, a Mexican badman, was even meaner when he had been drinking. About seven o'clock in the morning on July 8, 1882, Orante entered the saloon of Moses and Mehan, on the corner of Fifth and Fremont Streets in Tombstone, and loudly demanded a drink. He was already intoxicated and soon drew his pistol which he flourished in a threatening manner.

The barkeeper, James Hennessey, tried to get him to put his revolver away, but the Mexican was evidently in a dangerous mood, and only grew worse with an outburst of profanity and waving the pistol about.

Hennessey could see nothing but violence would come from Orante, so he dispatched a messenger to find an officer of the law and inform him of the proceedings at the saloon. The messenger found Kiv Phillips and that officer hastened to Moses and Mehans.

The barkeep explained the state of affairs to him. The Mexican had left the bar, but the barkeep told Phillips that he was armed and dangerous, and that he should use extreme caution, if approaching him.

Deputy Phillips went outside with the intention of disarming and arresting Orante.

As he approached, Orante stepped backward and stumbled; at the same time drawing his pistol and firing with deadly accuracy, the bullet striking the doomed officer in the right shoulder and passing through the wind-pipe, lodging in the vitals.

Simultaneously with the firing of that murderous shot, Phillips drew his own revolver and, though dying on his feet, fired a shot at his killer.

Then, with unbelievable tenacity of life, the mortally wounded Deputy turned and entered the saloon and, with blood gushing from his mouth, walked through the saloon and *out the back door,* a distance of some thirty steps, then fell dead.

The sound of the shots attracted the attention of Officer Harry Solon, who rushed to the scene and put the seriously wounded Orante under arrest. Solon commandeered an express wagon to haul the Mexican to jail. The shot, fired by the dying Phillips, struck the right thigh of Orante, knocking him down. When Dr. Goodfellow dressed the wound, he said that the bullet had also broken the hip-bone, passed through the rectum, inflicting a dangerous and, most likely, fatal wound. Goodfellow also said that his chances of recovery would be greatly improved if he was lodged in a place more suitable than the jail.

When word of the murder got out about town, a large crowd gathered in the streets of Tombstone and much talk about lynching the Mexican killer was bandied about.

Señor Corella, the Mexican Consul in Tombstone, notified Sheriff John Behan of the situation who, as a precautionary measure, placed extra guards about the jail.

While dressing Orante's wound, Dr. Goodfellow found the scars of four old bullet wounds on his body. He (Orante) said he was a native of Hermosillo, Sonora, and that he had come to Tombstone for the purpose of avenging the death of his countryman who, some time back, had shot and wounded Officer Poynton and had then been killed by Chief Neagle when he refused to surrender.

Dr. Goodfellow conducted a post-mortem examination of Officer Kiv Phillips and found the nature of his wounds to be as follows:

"The bullet entered the upper part of the right arm, passed through the pectoral muscles in front of the armpit, entered the chest cavity between the first and second ribs, then passed through the upper lobe of the left lung in the left side of which it lodged. Death occurred from hemorrhage into the windpipe and pleural cavities."

At the regular meeting of the Rescue Hook and Ladder Company, a committee was appointed to report resolutions of sympathy at the untimely death of Kiv Phillips, who was an honored member of the company. The committee was also instructed to take charge of the remains until the arrival of Phillips' brother.

A native of New York, and about twenty-six years old, Phillips had been in Tombstone for one year. He had acted as deputy clerk during the term of District Court and had won compliments from Bench and Bar for his excellent conduct and strict attention to the business at hand.

About four months earlier he had been temporarily employed by Sheriff Behan. The sheriff was so impressed with him that he retained him as a full time deputy.

Phillip's obituary said that he was a young man of most exemplary habits and good principles. That he was utterly devoid of fear in the discharge of his duty, though most quiet and unassuming in his manner. In short he was a true friend, an upright citizen, and an honest and capable officer.

The sad news was telegraphed to Ike Phillips, a brother of the deceased, of San Francisco.

He replied:

"Will leave tomorrow. Have the body embalmed."

The deceased had three brothers living in California, and a brother and sister in New York. The local paper on July 10, 1882, carried the following news item:

"THE MURDERED OFFICER

About noontime yesterday the remains of the late Kiv Phillips were taken from the undertaker's rooms on Allen Street and started on the journey to San Francisco. The body was not well embalmed and the stench was beginning to get so great that it

was feared the express company would not ship it. A detachment of about sixty men from the Hook and Ladder Company and forty from the Engine Company, under the command of Chief Engineer McCann, marched to the undertaker's rooms at half past eleven, and formed in double line, between which the wagon, containing the remains, passed: A procession was then formed in the following manner; Carriage carrying the remains, brass band playing funeral dirge, Hook and Ladder Company under the immediate command of Fireman Hatch, Engine Company No. 1, under command of acting Foreman Moriarity, carriages, and citizens on foot. The firemen and pedestrians accompanied the remains to the outskirts of the city, and several of the carriages went as far as Contention. The bell on Hook's truck house tolled sadly as the procession marched through the city, and a general feeling of sadness seemed to pervade the community. The order and decorum displayed by the firemen noticed and generally commended. It is supposed that the murdered man's brothers will meet the remains somewhere on the railroad and act as escort to San Francisco."

Orante lived four days, then, he too, cashed in his chips. The murderer was unceremoniously planted in Boothill.

REFERENCES:

1. *Tombstone Epitaph,* July 10, 1882.

2. Residents of Tombstone's Boothill, by Ben T. Traywick, Red Marie's Bookstore, 1971.

1883 — 1883

Tombstone A.T.

FUNERAL NOTICE.

Tombstone A T

THE FUNERAL OF

William Kinsman,

Deceased, will take place on Sunday, February 25th, at 1 o'clock p. m., from the residence of his parents, corner of Seventh and Toughnut streets.

Friends and acquaintances are invited to attend.

Killed by May Woodman

William Kinsman
Funeral Notice

15

MAY WOODMAN
A WOMAN SCORNED

At about 10:30am on February 23, 1883, William Kinsman was standing in front of the Oriental Saloon on Tombstone's Allen Street. Here, he was accosted by a very angry woman. After only a few words, she pulled out a .38 caliber revolver and, shot him point-blank.

The ball entered Kinsman's left side about four inches below the nipple and passed horizontally through the body. The woman attempted to fire a second shot into the prone body of her victim, but the weapon was struck down by Chief of Police Coyle, the ball entering the sidewalk.

When the woman was arrested by Chief Coyle, she claimed to have been driven to the act by abuse received from Kinsman with whom she had been living for some months. After her arrival at City Hall, she asked Constable Ike Roberts if she had hit Kinsman. Upon being informed that she had not only hit him, but probably had killed him, she seemed very satisfied.

Front of the Oriental Saloon
where May Woodman shot William Kinsman

Kinsman lived about four hours after being shot. He formerly lived in Virginia City. He was about twenty-five years old and was a well-known sporting man.

The fair-skinned woman was twenty-seven years old, named Mrs. May Woodman, and had come to Tombstone from Bodie some two years before. Jealousy was thought to be the reason she shot Kinsman.

A practical joker most likely caused this death. Someone placed an ad in the *Tombstone Epitaph* stating that William Kinsman intended to marry May Woodman. To correct this article, Kinsman placed a notice in the next issue that he had no intention of committing matrimony with May.

It is likely that when the woman read the rejection she deliberately set out to kill Kinsman.

At the trial, she testified that she had shot Billy in self defense. However, she was convicted of manslaughter. Before she was sentenced, she attempted suicide by taking chloral hydrate and morphine. Dr. Goodfellow was summoned in time to save her life. The explanation as to how she had procured this poison was:

"For some days a mixture of choral hydrate and morphine had been administered to produce sleep. This medicine, instead

of taking when administered by her attendants, she carefully saved until quite a quantity of the deadly drug had accumulated."

It was an explanation—not very acceptable—but... Dr. Goodfellow also discovered something else unknown about May.

In his medical report he stated that it was apparent that Kinsman or someone had beaten her even though she was pregnant.

There was no mention of these facts at her trial. She miscarried while in jail, and Dr. Goodfellow said that the fetus was at four or five months.

Most of the public in Tombstone took sides against May in the shooting. Even the *Epitaph* printed a brief line to that effect. It read:

"It is said that May Woodman, who is confined in the county jail awaiting trial for murder is insane. The conclusion has been arrived at from her recent actions."

On May 22, 1883, Judge Pinney overruled the motion for a new trial for May and sentenced her to five years in the penitentiary. The Judge informed the prisoner that her term could be utilized by her in preparation for a higher and better life. That the full limit of the law was a comparatively light sentence taken in connection with her crime, and he felt that his duty compelled him to sentence the prisoner to the term of five years, the utmost prescribed for the offense.

Upon receiving the sentence, May turned angrily to the judge and shouted, "May God curse you *forever!*"

Not long after May arrived at the Territorial Prison in Yuma, she became the center of another controversy. She was pregnant again. All the prison officials maintained that it was absolutely impossible for any male to gain access to the women's portion of the prison. With such as it may, the story was that the woman was pregnant and she certainly had not accomplished this feat all alone.

On November 24, 1883, the *Arizona Sentinel* wrote:

"If current reports be true, a scandal of some magnitude will be made public in connection with the territorial prison administration, the irrepressible May Woodman from Tombstone notoriety having become with child since her incarceration in that secluded retreat on the Colorado."

The *Sentinel* later reported:

"To ascertain the truth or falsehood of the statement made, (concerning May Woodman's pregnancy) author's words enclosed, a representative of the Sentinel visited the prison, and interviewed the prison authorities. Aside from the emphatic denial of the superintendent, the warden, and the woman herself, we are convinced that under the circumstances such a condition of affairs would be impossible. The woman is kept under as strict discipline as the rest of the prisoners, occupies a cell which is inaccessible from others, and the key of her cell, after locking up at night, is deposited in a safe to which no one has access except the turnkey. Of course, this report was started simply to injure Captain Ingalls, the superintendent of the prison and has no foundation except in the imagination of some brute to whom a pure thought is an absolute stranger."

Whether the accusations were true or false, acting Arizona Governor Van Arman was so dismayed at the turn of events, that he pardoned her on March 15, 1884, (she had served less than one year of her five year sentence), on the condition that she leave the Territory immediately and forever.

May Woodman accepted these terms and was pardoned. She took the first train to California and... *disappeared.*

REFERENCES:

1. *Arizona Daily Star,* February 25, 1883; May 26, 1883.

2. *Los Angeles Daily Times,* May 27, 1883.

3. *Arizona Daily Citizen,* May 25, 1883.

4. *Tombstone Epitaph,* February 23, 1883; August 25, 1883.

5. *Arizona Sentinel,* May 19, 1883; May 25, 1883; November 24, 1883.

6. *Globe Chronicle,* January 12, 1884; March 22, 1884.

7. Letters Requesting Pardon: Patrick Hamilton, Phoenix, Arizona, August 18, 1883.

8. Pardon and terms included: Executive Department, Office of the Governor, August 22, 1883.

9. Release Order: Yuma, Arizona Territory, F.S. Ingalls, Superintendent, March 15, 1884.

10. Yuma Quartermaster Depot Records, Arizona State Parks, Yuma Territorial Prison.

William Cornell Greene
Copper King of Cananea

16

Bill Greene
Copper King of Cananea

"Don't shoot me, Bill! I'm not armed!"

Despite the plea for mercy, four heavy .45 slugs blasted the life from Jim Burnett's body. Tombstone could chalk up another bloody killing!

It was July 1, 1897, and William Cornell Greene had just shot and killed *"Justice Jim"* (James) Burnett. The shooting took place on Allen Street at the entrance to the famed O.K. Corral.

When the City Marshal, Charley Wiser, heard the roar of the gunfire down on Allen Street, he headed there at a dead run.

He met Greene coming up Allen Street, gun dangling from his hand.

"You've killed *'Justice Jim,'*" the Marshal said.

"Yes, I had to kill him." Greene replied, giving the Marshal his gun.

"Justice Jim" Burnett had been a tough hombre who ran his Court in Charleston the way he saw fit. There are doubts as to how

he obtained his position as Justice of the Peace, but once he had established himself in office, his methods were unusual, to say the least.

After his first quarter in office, Jim dutifully made out his report and sent the fines he had collected to the Board of Supervisors in Tombstone. Along with his report, he sent a bill for three hundred eighty dollars as his percentage of the fines. Although his was a fee office, the supervisors felt this was too much and cut the amount considerably.

When this news reached Burnett, he sent word to the supervisors that his Justice Court in Charleston would look out for itself in the future.

True to his word, his court never asked anything of the county nor did he ever send it anything. Thereafter the court was conducted for the benefit of *"Justice Jim"* Burnett and for no other reason.

There was absolutely no red tape or legal delay in his court. Anyone who came before him was assumed guilty. The only decision to be made was the degree of guilt. He issued his own warrants whenever he needed them and, armed with six-gun and scatter gun, served them himself.

Anywhere, any time, and for any reason, he would convene court and dispense his brand of justice. His prime objective was to see that his court make a good profit.

Fines were adjusted to what the defendant could pay and just how much money Jim happened to need at that time. His decisions were prompt and the verdicts enforced by the business end of a six-gun. No appeal was allowed and *"Justice Jim"* collected the fines himself.

THE GREENE TRAGEDY

William Greene had gone to Tombstone early in the silver boom and built himself a ranch near Hereford. His family consisted of Mrs. Greene, who had been Mrs. Moson, two children, Frank and Virginia, both by her first husband, and two daughters, Ella, nine years old, and Eva, seven years old, the results of her marriage to Greene.

Ella was a beautiful child and well-liked by all who knew her. She was the pride of her father's life.

Greene had built a small dam on the San Pedro River, not far from his ranch. The purpose of this dam was to provide irrigation water for the alfalfa fields.

During the warm months of the year, the children from Greene's ranch swam in the river several hundred yards below the dam. The water was only about two and one-half feet deep at this spot and was considered safe for them.

Greene's nearest neighbor was Jim Burnett, whose ranch lay about a mile-and-a-half down the San Pedro. Burnett and Greene had no disagreement over the first dam that Greene built. However tempers flared when he imported a number of Chinese and began construction on a second one.

Scarcely had the new dam been completed when a mysterious explosion demolished it on June 24, 1897. The sudden release of water washed out great channels of rock and gravel from the river bed for a considerable distance downstream.

No one thought much about it on the evening of June 27, 1897, when Ella and Eva Greene announced that they were taking their friend, Katie Corcoran down to the swimming hole. After all, it was more of a wading spot than anything. The water was shallow and the children went there often. No one thought about the water that had been released when the dam was destroyed. The three little girls giggling at little girl antics, ran to the river.

Katie arrived there first and plunged in but, instead of finding shallow water and the familiar sandy bottom, she encountered only deep water. The Greene girls stared in fear and amazement as she disappeared from sight.

Ella jumped into the river in a vain attempt to rescue her friend. When she saw that she, too, was trapped in the deep water, she screamed to her littie sister, Eva, "No, Eva! Get back! *Get back!*"

Little Eva, terrified, ran to the ranch for help, but assistance arrived much too late. The day after the girls were drowned, Greene, wild with anger and shock, posted a notice in *the Prospector* to the effect that he would pay:

> ***"...$1,000 to anyone who could identify the person or persons who dynamited his dam and indirectly caused the death of the two girls."***

Somehow, in his distraught thinking, he placed the blame squarely on Jim Burnett. Thus when he saw *"Justice Jim"* leaving *"Honest John"* Montgomery's O.K. Corral, he pulled his six-gun and killed

Burnett. There is no doubt that *"Justice Jim"* committed numerous crimes and aided and abetted or condoned scores of others. Perhaps guilty of these, he was innocent of the one for which he paid the supreme penalty.

The investigation proved that he did not blow up Greene's dam. The Chinese, who were not familiar with the use of explosives, were the ones who destroyed the dam accidentally.

The verdict of the Coroner's Jury was:

"James C. Burnett, a resident of Pearce, 67 years of age, came to his death by four gunshot wounds inflicted by William C. Greene on July 1, 1897, at about 1:00 P.M. in the City of Tombstone."

Although Justice Duncan ruled that Greene be held without bail for the Grand Jury, Sheriff Scott White, a close friend of Greene, refused to lock him up.

The shooting created quite a sensation and Burnett's funeral, held at the C.B. Tarbell Undertaking Parlors, was attended by a large number of relatives, friends, and curious onlookers. Jim, at the time of his death, was serving as the Justice of the Peace in Pearce. He left a wife and two grown daughters.

The Grand Jury indicted Greene for murder in the second degree. To this charge he pled: "not guilty." The men selected to serve on the Jury were: Frank Ray, Thomas Fulgrum, Ernest Baker and James Kragbaum, James Blair, A.J. Cronk, R.W. Barr, Charles Fredericks, D.L. Hughes, A.M. Bradford, E.A. Wittig, and James Scow.

Colonel and Judge William Herring

Tombstone really boomed during the days of the trial. Gamblers along Allen Street raked in piles of money. The odds were about even that Greene would go free for the murder of Jim Burnett.

When the trial opened on December 17, 1897, Greene was confident that his many friends would help him win his case in any way they could, and that they did. There was a parade of Greene's friends to the witness stand each telling that Burnett had threatened Greene's life.

Bill Greene took the stand and testified that Ben Sneed had informed him that his dam had been dynamited by Chinese and Mexicans and that one Ab On had said it was done on Burnett's orders. All heresay testimony and by the defendant, but it carried an impact.

District Attorney Lord could find but one lawyer who would help him prosecute Greene. Colonel William Herring was the only other lawyer in Arizona who had not been bought by Greene's money. The accused had no desire to be the guest of honor at a neck-tie party so he used his fortune in any way he could. It was a costly legal battle, but Greene managed to save his neck. Although it was a clear miscarriage of justice, the jury let him go Scot free. His high-priced lawyers built such a case that the jury was only out ten minutes.

They ignored the fact that the accused had shot down an unarmed man and pronounced him *"not guilty!"*

It cost Greene a fortune to kill Jim Burnett as, for years after, he was still passing out money to the jurors who freed him.

Bill Greene had been a ruthless, fighting man all his life. At the age of eighteen, he had left Westchester County New York to come West with a Government surveying party.

He learned the business of copper mining the hard way: underground at the Wickenburg and Prescott mines, in 1877.

When Scout, Jack Dunn, found copper outcroppings in the Apaches' back yard down in the Mule Mountains, Greene went along to share in the wealth of *"red gold."*

It was 1887 before Greene got his opportunity. He had prospected through the Bradshaw Mountains with George Burbank when the Apaches were as thick as fleas. During the times that mining didn't pay his way he cut firewood in the Dragoon Mountains and sold it in Tombstone at fourteen dollars a cord. Thus, he knew the southern part of Arizona and northern Sonora well.

During one of his long prospecting trips, he rode through the Cananea Range. There he viewed, in amazement, several abandoned mining properties. For some strange reason, he was sure that these mines still held millions in copper.

The widow of General Pesquieros gave him an option on the mining claims she owned. Working the mine on a shoe string, Greene finally hit a vein of twenty percent copper ore.

One good look at what he had and George Mitchell of the United Verde in Jerome put up enough funds to start the mine's production. That was only the beginning. They still needed money—big money to swing into full development, so Bill went to New York.

Calling himself *"Colonel"* William C. Greene, he went the whole route in fancy dress and grand manner. Carrying great chunks of red native copper about with him, he expounded on the millions in *"red gold"* being made in Butte and Bisbee. He sold stock like hot cakes, but was careful to retain the controlling amount.

Back in Cananea, he installed a huge pipeline and pump to supply his mines with water. A branch line railroad was needed, but the Southern Pacific refused to build it.

Greene built it himself for five hundred thousand dollars. Several years later he declined an offer of two million dollars from Southern Pacific for that spur.

Then the big bubble burst. The mines ran out of ore. The company was broke, or so everyone thought, *except* Bill Greene. Taking a big gamble, he went East again to sell mining stock. He bought tools and equipment on credit as well as hired a private railroad car to take a group of potential backers to the Cananea mines.

The nervy gambler had bet everything he owned on a mine that had run out of ore.

Dame fortune still smiled upon him however, for when he reached Cananea with his crowd of moneyed people, his underground superintendent told him they had run into new veins of copper in almost every tunnel. It was unbelievable.

Millions of dollars poured in from the Cananea mines and Greene invested a large part of it in land and cattle. In no time at all his Ranchos de Cananea ran fifty-five thousand head of cattle, and had twenty four hundred saddle horses. The ranch covered four hundred thousand acres and was divided into seven parts. These holdings eventually became the Greene Cattle Company.

At the turn of the century Amalgamated Copper, in an attempt to control the copper market, tried to buy Greene out. When he refused to sell, they set out to break him.

The magnates had literature spread among the Mexican workers in Greene's Cananea mines to cause trouble. The ruse was successful and the miners went on strike, demanding higher wages.

While Greene tried to talk sense into them, someone took a shot at him from the crowd. Greene shot him dead.

Several thousand angry miners, well supplied with mescal by the trouble makers, swarmed on the town. They overran John Metcalf's lumber yard, set it on fire and killed Metcalf and his nephew. Advancing on the plaza, they burned the town as they went.

When the mob reached Greene, he was surrounded by eleven tough, American miners. All of them fired on the leader of the mob and literally blew him apart. Then Greene and his men piled into his big touring car and roared down the street guns blazing.

The streets were turned into a battleground. Greene wired Bisbee for help and Tom Rynning and his Arizona Rangers came to the rescue.

After two full days of bloodshed the famed Colonel Emilio Kosterlitzky and his Rurales rode into town. The Colonel ordered anyone who refused to stop fighting, shot on the spot.

Sixty men lay dead and over one hundred were wounded. The miners went back to their jobs and Greene raised their pay, so no one really won anything.

Bill Greene's world began to slowly crumble about him. In 1904, his wife died, leaving him alone. He buried her in Bisbee beside little Ella who drowned in 1897. Greene remarried in 1905, to a daughter of Frank Proctor, but he was never the same again.

By 1907, Wall Street had gone to work on him in earnest. Rumors were circulated that the stock in Greene's mine was worthless. Consequently, the fickle, investing public sold that stock, driving the price down. To combat the failure of his stock, Bill sold the Greene Cattle Company and threw the money in. The panic grew worse steadily and Greene's bank called for more money. The smaller mines went the way of the cattle company, bringing the total expenditures of the attempt to save his Cananea mines to twenty million dollars.

At last, the end was in sight, for Greene could raise no more funds. All his requests for loans were denied.

However, the "Trust" had not reckoned with the man that was Bill Greene. Once he had overcome the terrible urge to kill the men who caused his ruin, his mind began to function again.

He still had many powerful friends in Mexico and they would help.

His Mexican friends did help, giving him options on gold, silver, timber and ranch lands. Now Wall Street would know that they were in for a fight, for Bill Greene didn't know the word *"quit."*

But the master of fate was drawing closed the curtain on the fabulous life adventure that had begun on August 26, 1852, in Duck Creek, Wisconsin.

Bill had just emerged after a shave in a barber shop in Cananea. While he was climbing into his buggy, the matched team of thoroughbreds were spooked. He managed to get his hand on one rein, but that was not enough. The team ran away smashing the buggy against the rocks, throwing Bill out and fracturing his skull.

William C. Greene died five days later on August 5, 1911. Friends buried him in Cananea. Even his enemies would have admitted that Greene was one of the greatest brawlers of the West in the era when copper was king!

REFERENCE:

1. Copper King of Cananea, by Ben T. Traywick, Golden West, November 1970.

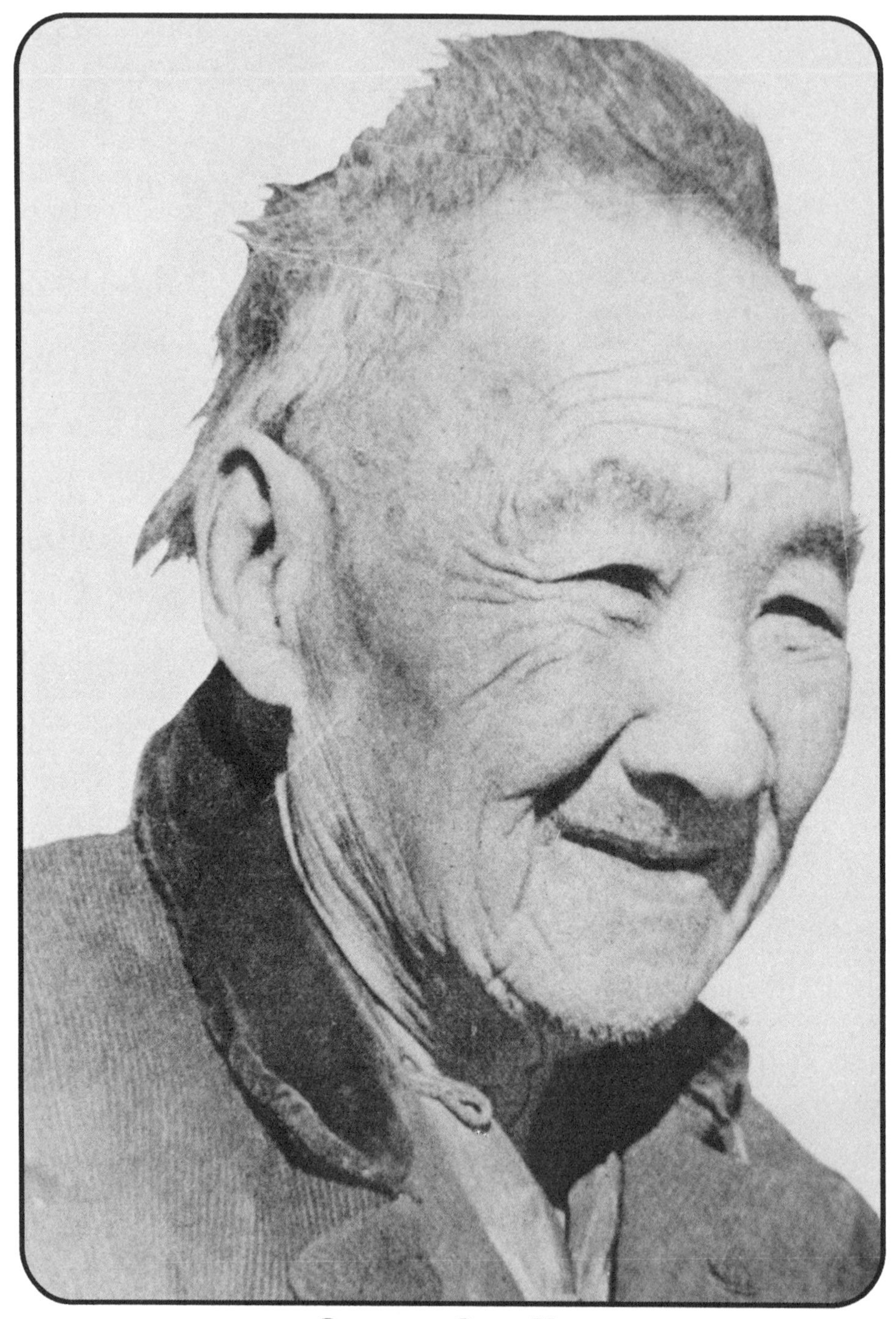

Quong Gee Kee
Co-owner of the Can Can Restaurant

17

Quong Gee Kee

Tombstone's Last Celestial

On a windy day in January, 1938, friends and relatives from Gleeson, Tombstone, Bisbee, Rain Valley, Douglas and Tucson, gathered at Boothill Cemetery to pay their final tribute to Quong Gee Kee, *Tombstone's Last Celestial.*

When the hearse arrived bringing Quong Kee to his place of eternal rest, over five hundred people stood around the open grave. Reverend Rupert Witt of St. Paul's Episcopal Church conducted the funeral services, although Quong was Chinese. Roland Bridges, Maine State Senator, delivered the eulogy at graveside, then quoted from the philosophy of Tao, the faith of Law Tzu, which was known six hundred years before the birth of Christ.

This funeral in Tombstone's famous Boothill was the first held there in thirty-two years. The last had been the burial of his old friend, China Mary, in 1905, beside whom he was to rest forever.

As the pallbearers lifted Quong's casket from the hearse, muted brass instruments lifted the strains of *"Abide With Me"* while the wind created a mournful dirge as it swept across the rocks and cacti of Boothill.

The minister began the funeral service in deep, clear, tones:

"Out of the deep, O' Lord, have I called unto Thee. We are gathered to do honor to a brother who has departed. We might call the life of Quong Kee the parable of the Good Chinaman for this man we bury has lived a life of service to the needy. Quong Kee turned no one away hungry."

"There is a Chinese proverb which reads 'A Chinese lies without regret if there is one man in all the world who calls him friend.' Quong must have died happy knowing that he had many friends."

"Nearer, My God, to Thee" sounded across the rocky hill as hundreds of people filed by the open casket for a last look at *"Old Quong."* Once the casket was closed and lowered into the grave, the crowd began to drift away. Quiet reigned for a short while, then there was the sound of failing clods. An era had come to an end in Tombstone.

It is true that other Chinese may one day live in Tombstone, but there will not be one who remembers the Earps and the Clantons, Doc Holliday, *"Curly Bill,"* Ringo, *"Big Nose"* Kate, or China Mary. It will not be one who was a part of the rise and decline of this famed silver camp, *"The town too tough to die."*

Quong's pallbearers were an unusual collection of individuals:

Dave O'Neal
Chairman of the State Tax Commission, Phoenix

John Gleeson
Founder and resident of Gleeson;

J.W. Smith
G.J. McCabe
George Berger,
all residents of Tombstone;

Gee Hing
of Rain Valley.

Two of Quong's countrymen, Gee Hing of Rain Valley and Yee Wee of Gleeson, were present at the funeral rites and said they were cousins to the deceased.

The crowd on Boothill that day was unusual to say the least. There were numerous school children, who had known and loved old Quong. In addition there were several Tombstone pioneers who had shared the wild, hectic days of the silver boom town with Quong. In those days burials in Boothill were practically a daily occurrence.

Historians disagree over Quong's birthplace. Some say Hong Kong and others say Canton. At any rate, he arrived from Hong Kong in the days when Virginia City, Montana was a boom town and found a job as a cook's helper.

He knew members of the Plummer Gang when they were believed to be respectable citizens.

Quong was also present the day that Plummer and his men were hanged by the Vigilantes, thus avenging the many deaths in that lusty, bawdy camp. The old Chinaman remembered much of those early days.

"Virginia City, he plenty wild. All time somebody getting lobbed; somebody getting killed. The Vigilantes, he come. You savvy Vigilantes? They catch lobbas, hang 'em all. One time five in one day! Then, Virginia City, he not be wild no more."

As Virginia City became a ghost town, the Union Pacific began laying ribbons of shining steel across the country. Quong fed the workers along the way and watched, with Oriental detachment, the monumental undertaking.

"Lailload man," he said, "work plenty damn hard all time. Lotsa work in good and bad weather. On pay day all get drunk and laise plenty hell!"

Quong was in the crowd that watched the Golden Spike driven, thereby uniting the nation.

Stockton, California grew into a teeming metropolis shortly after the railroad reached it. Eager to make his fortune, Quong opened a restaurant there. Much of the money that came into his hands, he put aside for his return to China.

"Stockton plenty busy," Quong once remarked. "Lotsa people all time hurry here, hurry there. Lotsa money. Lotsa business. Stockton good place. Lotsa 'yellow boys' there too. All work on lailload."

When he concluded his business venture in Stockton, Quong made a trip back to Hong Kong. He stayed for eight months. During that time he married and bought a home. Quong was looked upon with respect and awe as a man who was a world traveler and possessed much wealth. By the time he had lived in China a few short months, Quong decided to go back to the American West and make enough money so that he could live the rest of his days in China in comfort.

His wife bore him a son soon after his departure. Quong was never able to return to his beloved China and never was to see his son, who died in 1936 at the age of sixty.

Upon his return to America, Quong went to Willcox, Arizona, a rapidly growing cattle center in the 1870's. Again, he opened a restaurant appropriately called the *"Hindquarter."*

Here the men of the range: cowboy, rancher, and cattle buyer, could be fed an incomparable meal.

Of the cowboy, Quong said, "When he sober, cowpunch allight. When he drunk, cowpunch alla time laise hell!"

The reputation of Quong's food spread, business was booming and the enterprising Oriental began to expand. While the *"Hindquarter"* was prospering, Tombstone, a new boom town was coming into its own.

Quong could not resist the lure of the new boom town, and imme-

Building the railroad into Tombstone

The "Can-Can" Restaurant
owned by Quong Kee and his partner, Ah Lum.

diately moved there. He bought Ah Sing's share of the soon-to-be-famous *"Can-Can,"* and became Ah Lum's partner. This was soon followed by the *Grecian Restaurant* in Charleston. A few years later, Quong opened up the *Black Diamond Restaurant* in the Pearce vicinity.

Tombstone, the wild, new camp that had a man for breakfast every day, had sprung up over night. It lived fast and furious. Some struck it rich, and others

Wake Benge, Tal Roland & Jeff Lewis, some of the cowboys that came up with Slaughter's herds

gambled, drank, and robbed. Shooting up the town was a common form of amusement.

But Quong's breakfast consisted of steak and potatoes, ham and beans, and frequently eggs and coffee.

He, like all Orientals, showed little interest in the shootings, knifings, and gun battles. Cowman and rustler, lawman and gunfighter, gambler and miner; they all were customers at the *"Can-Can."*

One time, a horde of wild cowboys descended on the *"Can-Can"* after long months of isolation on the range. Five of them started to dismantle the place, terrifying the customers. They fled, along with the cooks and waiters. Quong returned to find his restaurant a shambles. Highly amused at Quong's display of temper, the cowpunchers completed the destruction of the *"Can-Can"* interior.

Many of Quong's friends advised him to have the culprits arrested, but the Chinese refused.

"Quong no allest them." he reasoned. "When cowpunch sober up, he solly for cause trouble. He come back and pay up. If Quong allest them, he lose five friends....good customers. Cowpunch get mad....never pay." About a week later, one of the cowboys returned to the *"Can-Can"* and approached Quong shame-faced.

"We acted like a bunch of fools the other night," he said, "Me and the boys would like to pay for busting up your place."

Quong told him the cost of the damages and the cowboy paid up. Quong was paid his damages and kept his friends and customers, too.

In the last years of his life, when Quong was asked about Tombstone gunmen, he would reply, "Aiee, I remember Wyatt Earp. He nice fella. Alla time eat at Quong's. Lotsa time he hard on other people. Sometime he shoot 'em up."

"Billy Clanton, he nice fella, always eat at *"Can-Can."* Nice boy...always pay his bill. Too bad he shot down in O.K. Corral."

"*'Cully Bill'* also good friend to Quong. Laugh lots, eat lots, pay bill quick. Quong hear talk that *'Cully'* badmans, lustler. You savvy lustler? *'Cully'* never bad to Quong. Quong *no have cows!"*

Quong Kee remembered the famous and the notorious of Tombstone. He knew them all and could tell the story and the end of many; the ones who had moved on elsewhere when the boom ended, and the ones who had remained beneath the rocky mounds on Boothill.

However, the golden days were over. The mines closed, people drifted away, and Tombstone rapidly became a ghost town. Quong's restaurants in Pearce, Charleston, and Tombstone "go bust" as he had more money on the books than in the till.

The old Chinaman never sued for his money. His explanation was, "No go to court. When they have money they pay. In court, lawyer take money. Then Quong have no money, no friends."

During his last years, Quong Kee was a picturesque figure on the streets of Tombstone.

A little dog usually followed the aged Chinese about. The twilight years of his life were spent on county charity and the aid from friends.

A few years before his death, the old Chinese gave up hope of ever returning to China. Papers found in his possessions, revealed a Federal Certificate of Residence, which was signed in Willcox in March 1894, giving his age as forty-two. This would have made him eighty-six at the time of his death.

Quong Kee believed, and always maintained, he was ten years older than that, thus making him ninety-six!

Marshal Hal Smith missed seeing Quong on the streets one day and entered the old man's living quarters, behind Nellie Cashman's Hotel, to investigate. He found him unconscious on the floor.

An ambulance rushed him to the hospital in Douglas, but the old fellow died at 2:00am.

Then, strange events began to take place.

For some obscure reason, Quong's body was rushed to Bisbee and buried in the Evergreen Cemetery.

Before his Tombstone friends knew that he was dead, he was already buried.

Scarcely had the burial been completed when Marshal Smith called Douglas to inquire about Quong. When he spread the word about Tombstone, everyone was quite indignant because Quong was considered so friendless that he was buried in a pauper's grave in a city strange to him. Within hours a sizable fund to "bring Quong home" was collected.

Quong was laid to rest with the men of the Old West; men he had known. On that rocky hillside, he lies among friends. He knew them much better than he knew his family and is more at home with them than with his ancestors.

His grave is beside that of China Mary, wife of Ah Lum, which was in accord with a request made by Quong. He was quoted as saying he would sleep more peacefully if his old friend, China Mary, was close by.

One old-timer was present who had been a mule skinner during Tombstone's heyday. He remarked,

"I guess old Quong had just about the biggest funeral ever held on Boothill. I've seen about fifty folks buried up here, and not one of them ever had any five hundred people turn out to see them get planted. It was far superior to any planting I ever watched there, even better than any Democrats."

Mike Coffee reminded the oldsters that they had forgotten the roast goose. In years gone by, the Chinese would provide a fine meal for a funeral. It was placed on the grave so that their departed brother could dine well on his journey to join his ancestors. Roast goose seemed to be the favorite dish.

By early morning of the next day the meal at Boothill had always completely disappeared. The recently departed didn't feast on it, however. Local Mexican kids caught on pretty quickly. They would thoroughly enjoy the Chinese feast.

Yee Wee, a Chinaman from Gleeson, said,

"Quong, he tleated Tombstone alla light. Now Tombstone treat Quong alla light. He fine fellow, Quong Kee."

One last remark was,

"Old Quong belongs right where he is. These around him were his friends when he was alive. He'll get along with them now all right, wherever they may be."

Surely, had Quong been able to see the funeral Tombstone gave him, he would have smiled his toothless smile and said,

"Ple–t–t–y damn nice!"

The life of Quong Kee was also the story of the West, the saga of the boom towns, the tough and roaring rail camps, the clinking of chips, the roar of guns in the mining and cow towns, and now, the men of the boom towns sleep the sleep of ages on Boothill.

It is no doubt proper, that Quong Kee lies among them . . .

REFERENCES:

1. *Arizona Highways,* July, 1949.

2. Bird Cage Theatre Museum files.

3. *Journal of Arizona History,* Arizona Historical Society, Autumn 1980.

4. The Residents of Tombstone's Boothill, by Ben T. Traywick, Red Marie's Bookstore, 1971.

5. *Arizona Daily Star,* January 16, 1938.

6. *Arizona Republican,* January 13, 1938.

China Mary
Wife of Ah Lum

Photo courtesy of the Chinese Benevolent Society

18

The Chinese In Tombstone

In the middle of the 18th century, M. DeGuignes astounded the entire scientific world when he reported to the Academy of Inscriptions and Belles Lettres in Paris that he had made a startling discovery in ancient Chinese historical records.

The writings revealed that five Buddhist Priests had found, and explored, a country called *"Fu Sang"* in the 5th century. DeGuignes' report stated that he believed *"Fu Sang"* to be none other than the Pacific Coast of America.

DeGuignes' statements were published in 1761, in the *Memoirs of the Academy at Paris.* The publication was entitled:

"Re' charches sur les Navigations des Chinois du Cote' de l'Amerique."

As expected, this publication created an abundance of excitement; America discovered by the Chinese one thousand years before Columbus! It was beyond belief!

Among the ancient hand-written records of China, there is an account of a Buddhist Priest who returned to China in 458 A.D. after a voyage lasting forty-one years. This was in the first year of the reign Yung–Yuen of the Emperor Tung Hwan–ban of the Tsi Dynasty.

This Buddhist Priest was called Hwui Shan. He claimed that he had been to a country that lay an unbelievable distance to the East.

When he told his amazing story to Government officials, Yu Kie, the Imperial Historiographer, who recorded the happenings and occurrences of the time, was so impressed that he made a complete record of the story told by Hwui Shan for the official records.

Ma Twan Lin, one of China's greatest scholars, rewrote those records into his voluminous writings.

Hwui Shan was able to convince the Chinese Emperor and scholars of that day, as well as the Chinese people, that he had, indeed, made such a voyage. In fact, he convinced them so well that, after fifteen centuries, almost every Japanese, Chinese, and Korean knows of Hwui Shan's visit to the Land of *"Fu Sang."*

The knowledge that Hwui Shan possessed about that part of the world where America lies could have been obtained only through having been there.

DeGuignes found, during his research of the Chinese archives, that there had been an extensive work called,

"The Description of Western Countries, in Sixty Volumes with Forty Books of Pictures and Maps."

This work was edited and written by many official writers from the memoirs of the most distinguished religious and secular authors. It was published in the year 666 A.D. by Imperial Decree, with an introduction by Emperor Kao-Thsang.

Only one copy was made because of the fantastic expense. This copy was kept in the Royal Palace in Peking. This valuable work and masses of other priceless historical material have disappeared since World War II.

Hwui Shan's forty-one-year voyage was also in detail in the Forty-First Book of Chuan in the 230th Volume of the:

"Great Chinese Encyclopedia"

It was gathered and issued as a publication by Emperor Liang's Court Historians from 502 to 556 A.D.

A vivid description of four principal places he visited during the voyage is given by Hwui Shan. Logically reasoning, these four places can be identified as:

(1) ***"Wenochin"*** was in the Kuriles Islands, probably Jesso;

(2) ***"Tahan"*** was the southern tip of Siberia, likely Kamchatka;

(3) ***"Fu Sang"*** was a place in California; and

(4) The ***"Kingdom of Women"*** could be no place but Mexico. His description of these women fit exactly the monkey, *Genus Hapole,* found nowhere else in the world except Southern Mexico.

Looking at a map, it is easily seen that the voyage through the island chains to America would have been quite simple for the bold and skillful Chinese sailors. They would have been scarcely out of sight of land during the entire trip. Hwui Shan's party left from Leaotong, the Northern Province of China.

He said,

"Fu Sang lies 20,000 li and more east of the Great Han country; also east of the Middle Kingdom."

From the mouth of the Hoang-Ho to the coast of North America, by a direct route East, is 20,000 Li or sixty-five hundred to seven thousand miles.

In Mexican history, there exists a tradition of Hwui Shan, bhikshu, as Wishi Pecocha and tells of his landing on the Pacific Coast; describes his complexion and dress; relates the doctrines he preached and why he returned to Asia after so many years. Tales also tell of the four Buddhist Priests who accompanied him. They became separated from him and never returned to China.

Author's Note:

"The story thus far has been to give some background to the Chinese people. Europe did not discover China. China discovered Europe and most likely America."

All the Chinese emigrants came to America under a system of contract which paid their passage, and for which they were to labor for a stated term. The business of hiring them out and governing their affairs was controlled by Chinese companies, to which they owed faith and fealty.

So many of the Chinese came to America that the number of these Chinese companies increased to six, and they soon came to be called, *"The Six Companies."*

They were all distinctly separate but operated on the same principles. All had the same laws and customs, such as their idolatry, worship of ancestors, and the obligations to the Chinese dead.

Death was never feared by the Chinese because of this company obligation. Each Chinese had the promise of *"The Six Companies"* that their bones would be returned to China for burial. Consequently, after a Chinese death, the sickening stench of burning flesh could be smelled in the Chinese section. The bones were scraped clean, wrapped in cloth or paper and sealed in zinc-lined boxes for shipment to China.

In the 1870's, Collis P. Huntington built a southern transcontinental railroad through Arizona. Hundreds of Chinese were employed in the construction of this railroad. When the railroad was completed, these Chinese settled in nearby towns. A few settled in with the local Indian tribes and some took new Spanish names and became vaqueros.

The new town settlers found employment as woodcutters, miners, charcoal manufacturers, vegetable gardeners, cooks, servants, and laundry men.

Several hundred Chinese settled in Tombstone during the silver boom. These particular Chinese seemed to be predominately from the Sam Yap and Sze Yap areas of China.

The Chinese were first regarded with open suspicion by the people of Tombstone, mainly due to their unusual cultural traits. The *"round eyes"* just did not understand that peach blossoms brought long life and that white narcissus flowers brought good fortune; nor that the queue worn by the Chinese men was a sign of loyalty to the Ch'ing Dynasty of Manchuria, which dominated all China from 1644 to 1911; nor that Chinese men were pleased by the bound feet of their women, signifying that a woman's position was in the home and that she should stay there.

To the white people, such a practice was simply the cruel and intentional maiming of helpless young girls.

Saloon keepers, store keepers, and gamblers bitterly opposed the Chinese. True, the Chinese had vices, such as opium and gambling, but even then, their money went to other Chinese.

Ill-will toward the Chinese first began because all of them lived and dressed just as they had in China. They did not patronize the local businessman any more than was absolutely necessary. All their clothing and food, mostly rice, they imported from China. They spent nothing except for the bare necessities of life.

Therefore, it was easy for the people of Tombstone to come to the conclusion that the Chinese were of no value to the town, or even to the country. Since they contributed nothing to the community, they were soon considered a public nuisance.

All in all, the Chinese were hard working, frugal, and there were no Chinese tramps or bums. Still they were not considered desirable citizens. Their quarters smelled of filth, were overcrowded, and they maintained all their Asiatic customs, and hated the "white devils," among whom they lived.

That is understandable, considering some of the treatment they received. However, even by Tombstone standards, the Chinese were highly immoral, selling their women and female children, exercising a system of female slavery.

The Chinese section of Tombstone was called *"Hoptown"* by the "roundeyes" and it extended from Third Street, west to First Street and from Fremont Street south to Toughnut and below.

All the Chinese lived in this area that was honey-combed with underground tunnels, gambling and opium dens. Dusk always brought the sweet odor of opium to the evening breeze.

Frequently, a large shipment of exotic food arrived from China, at which time the *"Hoptown"* Chinese always had a huge feast.

One such feast was described as,

"...having forty courses and consisting partly of Chinese brandy, rat pot pie, birds' nest soup, roasted puppy dogs with caterpillar sauce, roast baby chicks, shark tails stewed in India ink, veal cutlets, stuffed gull heads, monkey hands fried in

marrow, kittens fried in batter, worm chowder, turnip juice, pigs eyes' pudding; and lizard on toast, plus many other delicacies to make a delightful repast, at least to the Chinese.

Chinese emigrants brought Old China to Tombstone with them. Although they lived their lives there, raised their children and died there, they steadfastly kept to life and worship just as their ancestors had for thousands of years.

Their head-quarters or *"Joss House,"* lavishly decorated with mahogany and teak woods, brass, gold, and jade carved idols of ancient Chinese gods and goddesses, and embroidered trappings symbolized how much of ancient China was in Tombstone.

ANTI-CHINESE MOVEMENT APPEARS

On the night of July 24, 1880, banners and bonfires were prominent along Allen Street between Fifth and Sixth Streets where the first Anti-Chinese meeting was being held. A ten man committee was appointed to inform the local Chinese of their decision that:

"John Chinaman must go!"

When confronted with this declaration, the Celestials adopted a tough stance and said they would go when they were good and ready. One Chinese said he would go back to China when the white men paid him the seven hundred dollars they owed him.

Another said,

***"I got money—you no got money.
I go China, you go hell!"***

At the next anti-Chinese meeting a speaker told the assemblage:

"No means save violence can be devised for rooting out the pest and as that was not for a moment contemplated, the matter had better be dropped."

The Anti-Chinese League seemed to disappear after that.

Almost all the Chinese smoked opium. This drug was smuggled in from China through the mail, sealed in tins labelled "tobacco," and in large jars labelled *"tea."* There were many dens where a user could go and inhale the powerful drug until he reached a stupefied condition, complete with heavenly visions and exciting imaginary experiences.

A Tombstone newspaper reporter described his visit to a local *"opium den"*:

"I went through a small hole used as a door; entered a series of rooms used for gambling and smoking opium. In one room there was just one smoked, begrimed lamp burning. There were some mine bunks, built in tiers, as berths on a ship. Each bunk contained a man or woman smoking opium."

"The opium was in a little bone box and the smokers would take a wire and dip it into the box and then hold it over the flame of the lamp until it resembled a little round ball about the size of a pea. This they would push into the bowl of a pipe and take about half a dozen whiffs and then repeat the dose from one to half dozen times."

"About then the pipe would drop from their fingers and they would succumb to the effects of the drug and dream of elephants with calico tails and magnificent mansions in China, with high walls around them and through which gates Marshal Coyle and his officers could never enter and disturb them while shooting firecrackers or hitting the pipe."

These opium dens sprang up in the most unlikely places, only to have the local law raid them. Even while the marshal was in the process of raiding, preparations by the Chinese were underway to open another one at a different location.

During its zenith, *"Hoptown"* had Chinese gambling halls, restaurants, mercantile stores, barber shops, and *"Houses of Ill-Repute."*

A Chinese, named Sam Hing, owned and ran the Bird Cage Laundry in an old building next to the Bird Cage Theatre. Another Chinese laundry man was Yee Yee, who had six fingers on each hand. He had his laundry next door to Schieffelin Hall, and though it changed hands several times, it remained a laundry until 1930. The last owner was Wong Dee Hong.

In the Ivey Block, an old Chinese merchant ran a fine general store filled with articles inlaid with silver, glassware, toys, etc. This old man's young wife produced a set of twins. Set in the old ways of China, this new father had some peculiar ideas. He firmly believed that if a heathen American ever looked upon his wife's face, then she would be defiled forever. Consequently, no non-Oriental in Tombstone ever saw her face.

Shortly after the birth of the twins, he decided to send his family back to China. A carriage was hired to take them to the railroad in Benson. There was a large crowd of the curious, who had gathered to see their departure.

The old merchant came first, leading his wife, who was quite obviously much younger, and dressed in tight-fitting black with a veil covering her face. Following were Ah Lum and China Mary, each carrying one of the twins. It was quite a procession, even for Tombstone.

It was unusual for any of the Chinese to be involved in any gunfight, particularly with one of the "white devils" but it did happen on October 22, 1900. Stephen Ruff, rancher, gambler, and sometimes would-be badman, was refused a meal in the Chinese Restaurant on Allen Street. Sam Chung refused him because he was already indebted to Chung for four meals.

Ruff, who had been drinking earlier, abused and threatened the Chinaman. He left the restaurant but returned in a short while armed with a six-shooter and Winchester. Again he asked for a meal and again Chung refused.

An argument ensued and spilled out into the street in front of Yaples Store, Chung was following Ruff shouting epithets at him. The Chinese grabbed a gun from a passerby and opened fire on Ruff. The Oriental's accuracy was uncanny, as he hit Ruff three times, once through the heart and two through the intestines, missing only one of his four shots.

Ruff managed to get off only one shot, but that one blasted through Chung's left lung, and passed through his body exiting near the spinal column. Stephen Ruff was killed instantly, while Sam Chung died a short time later.

A Coroner's Jury rendered the verdict that Ruff met his death by gunshot wounds at the hands of one Sam Chung, and that the killing was justifiable homicide, having acted in self defense. Public sentiment on the streets agreed.

The Epitaph also added,

> ***"Ruff, formerly the foreman of the Erie Cattle Company, was a quiet citizen - but when in his cups is claimed to be of a quarrelsome disposition. The Chinaman was industrious and peaceable and it is most unfortunate."***

G.W. Chapman, known as *"Old Chap,"* was, for several years, an express messenger and mail clerk and held many responsible positions in Tombstone during its early days. He was a most honest, efficient officer.

In 1882, *"Old Chap"* was express and mail agent between Yuma and Los Angeles. *"Old Chap's"* train often carried the bones of dead Chinese from Arizona to the Golden Gate for shipment home to China. This traffic was particularly disagreeable to him.

One day, while the train was moving slowly across the bridge from Yuma, *"Old Chap"* was standing in the open door of the express car which contained several of these objectionable defunct Chinese bodies. The day was warm and the odor not pleasant and *"Old Chap"* was indignant. Seizing hold of the boxes, he dumped the whole shipment into the Colorado River and the bones of the Celestials are probably still floating in the Gulf of California far from their Oriental home.

"Old Chap" was fired, of course. A few years later he was the Republican candidate for the City Assessor of Tombstone, and the Democratic paper charged him with dumping the Chinese bones.

"Old Chap" took the bull by the horns, acknowledging it publicly saying, "Yes, I did dump the *d--n* Chinamen into the river; and if I had it to do over again, I would throw every *d--n* Chinaman, alive or dead, into the Colorado River that came to Arizona."

This answer caught the people and Chapman got the largest majority of any man that ever ran on any ticket in the City of Tombstone.

The Tombstone Prospector also carried various and sundry articles on the local Chinese. One such was the obituary of Wong Fat:

> ***"'Wong Fat, he die las' night all leddy!' This was the announcement made by Sam Lung this morning. Wong Fat's death was deplorable in the extreme - he, being in tbe prime of life, 98 years of age. Wong's people are distinguished for longevity. They don't cut their teeth 'till they are 72. Wong took his first breath in the far away flower kingdom 98 summers ago in October."***
>
> ***"Wong Fat may line up at the eternal roll call, don his fez with red tassel on it, tune up his one string fiddle, and tighten up his tom-tom to the tune of everlasting praise to the author of his immortality. It is custom to cover the dead Mongolian's grave***

with roast pig and other delectable viands which accounts for the manner in which the pelados manage to live all year round in camps and cities where a high born Chink occasionally departs this life."

"Bye Bye Wong Fat."

Author's Note:

"It is quite an unusual obituary and one that certainly verifies that the reporter knew little about the Chinese people."

Another article appeared:

"On February 1st, the Tombstone contingent of Chinamen will celebrate Chinese New Year. A local Celestial volunteered the information that beginning that day the China New Year will be the year 4605."

"The Chinese are very systematic and all arrange to be born on New Year's Day. If any of them has been so careless as to come into the world a few days or months late or early, he rectifies the error by counting only from New Year's Day of the year in which he was born. A birthday present and a New Year's present can thus be rolled into one."

Author's Note:

"Very few references are found that substantiate that the Chinese in Tombstone did have a Masonic Lodge. Again, the old files of the Prospector come to the rescue."

As published by *the Prospector:*

"CHINESE MASONS
A BRANCH OF MYSTIC
ORGANIZATION IN TOMBSTONE"

"The Chinese Masonic Lodge of Tombstone has been carrying on high jinks the past few days. They have been at work initiating a number of candidates into the mysteries of the order, who came from Pearce, Lewis Springs, and other places. The festivities will continue for several days. Ceremonies are being held in the second story of the King Building on the corner of Third and Allen Streets. A big feast will wind up the work of the lodge."

Again *the Prospector* speaks to describe the return of Chinese bones to China for burial:

***"CHINAMEN IN U.S.
SHIPPING CORPSES BY WHOLESALE
QUEER CUSTOM OF CELESTIALS
MANY SKELETONS SENT FROM ARIZONA"***

"Vessels leaving San Francisco for Chinese ports during the next month or two will carry back to the land of the dragon many shipments of the bones of departed Chinamen, several bodies having been sent from Arizona - and one is reported sent from Tombstone."

"According to the religious notions of the Chinese the souls of the departed will not be allowed to enter Paradise until the bodies are buried in the fatherland, and this belief has given rise to a profitable business to the various trans-Pacific steamship companies."

"The bodies of the dead are wired together, labelled, and placed in caskets prior to shipment to relatives or friends in China. The corpse agencies are required to guarantee that not a bone will be missing as only a complete skeleton is allowed to enter the heaven of the Chinese."

Another article told of a beautiful Chinese girl, about fifteen or sixteen years old, who arrived in Tombstone from San Francisco to visit relatives. She was said to be extremely good looking and attracted considerable attention. One of her many attractions was a brilliant red queue which the privilege of wearing was allowed to only a select few young and unmarried females, according to ancient Chinese customs.

Still another article told of a Chinese barbecue. It said that:

"...the entire Oriental population turned out with a roasted hog, and all the other delicacies peculiar to the Chinese. They, then, proceeded to their cemetery (Boothill) where, instead of consuming the feast that they brought, they consecrated it to their dead."

Comment was also made that:

"...a crowd of small Mexican boys trailed after the procession and that unless the departed Celestial spirits made haste with their offered feast, they might well go hungry for another year."

The Daily Prospector of February 27, 1890, carried an article of great interest to historians:

"The Can-Can Restaurant will remove to the corner of Allen and Fourth streets opposite the C.H. & T. Co.'s store on or about March 15."

On October 22, 1898, *the Prospector* carried another item on the Can-Can:

"A CELESTIAL ACCUSED OF ROBBING A SAFE"

"Last night Mr. Ah Wing, an almond-eyed celestial gentleman, who presides over the dish washing department of the Can-Can Restaurant, was arrested by Chief of Police Wiser and booked on a charge of burglary being strongly suspected of robbing the Can-Can safe on the night of the 11th inst. and pocketing about $500."

On October 26th *the Prospector* carried an item that declared that Ah Wing had been released as there was no case to be made out against him.

The Epitaph of January 23, 1897, made mention of the Oriental New Year:

"Chinese New Year was ushered in about 12 o'clock last night by a fusillade of firecrackers and bombs and our Celestial denizens will continue to make noise enough during the holidays to keep the devil away from the entire city."

The Prospector of August 14, 1897, told of Chinese deportations:

"Toy Wong, Wong Song, and Wong Fong, the three Chinamen taken to Tucson from Tombstone by Customs Inspector, Bob Hannah and charged with being in the country unlawfully, were taken before Judge Davis there, and after hearing the evidence, all three were ordered deported to China via San Francisco."

The Epitaph of July 17, 1898, described the funeral of the murdered Chinese vegetable peddler:

"Sing He, the murdered Chinaman was buried yesterday from the undertaking parlors of C.B. Tarbell. As the deceased and his partners were more or less Americanized in customs, the funeral was conducted somewhat on orthodoxal lines. The hearse was followed by a wagon load of belongings of the deceased. When the Chinese cemetery was reached and the casket lowered, the friends of the departed each drank some Chinese wine and, in turn, offered a short prayer. Then their attention was turned to burning the worldly effects of the deceased; blankets, clothing, garments, papers, jewelry, etc., even one half sack each of barley and wheat was sacrificed to the flames. The usual ostentation and pageantry of Chinese funerals was absent. No banquet of suckling pigs and side dishes were provided and other details avoided."

On May 16, 1897, *the Prospector* carried a vivid article of a Chinese marriage:

"CHINESE UNITED IN MARRIAGE BY THE AMERICAN PROCESS"

"Happy Yip Sun and Miss Lum Yup, two natives of the flowery kingdom, the former a prosperous merchant of this city, and the latter a dove-eyed damsel with very small feet, a token of the noble blood that courses through her veins, were united in marriage last night. The ceremony was not according to the orthodox Chinese belief, but was performed under the laws of Arizona. Probate Judge Crouse, in pigeon (sic) English, spoke the words that made Yip Sun the lord and master of the fair flower of far-off China."

"The bride was timid and acted like a frightened fawn when the judge ranged her long side of her future husband."

The judge had recourse to that winning smile, which is part stock in trade of a county school superintendent and under its influence the maid lost her timidity and naively smiled back at the judge. The conclusion of the ceremony was the commencement of the celebration in honor of the event, and the assembled Mongolian guests showered compliments on the groom, but took no notice of the bride, who shrank into a corner and took no part in the festivities."

Because Tombstone had a reputation for sudden, bloody occurrences, most men went armed - many Chinese citizens included.

Foo Kee, Tombstone candy store owner was stabbed to death in his own store just after the turn of the century.

His store was located where the Wagon Wheel Restaurant Bar now stands.

Author's Note:

"Twenty years ago a painting was located on this floor depicting Foo Kee as he lay dead."

On the day of his death, Foo Kee was happily involved in an opium session with his good friend, Wing Lung. During the session, a number of young boys burst into the store disrupting the Chinamen's party.

When the boys saw what was happening, they decided to have some fun with Foo Kee. They began to scatter his wares around the shop and when Foo objected to such actions they began to push him around, too. Wing Lung reached into his long Oriental robes and came out with a slender dagger.

Going to the aid of his friend, Wing slashed the hand of one of the boys, who had raised the hand in self-defense. A fierce struggle ensued in the tiny, cramped quarters.

In the fight, Wing stabbed at the boys again, but lost his balance and his long, sharp dagger pierced the heart of his friend, Foo Kee. Wing immediately realized he had killed his best friend, the man he tried to defend. As soon as they realized that a tragedy had occurred, the boys fled.

During the restoration of the Wagon Wheel several years ago, workmen found a number of clay pots and opium pipes under the very spot of the store owned by Foo Kee. Foo Kee was buried in the Chinese section of Tombstone's Boothill.

Wing Lung never recovered from his sorrow in killing his best friend.

There is no evidence in the city records that he was prosecuted for the act or even arrested for that matter.

He just vanished among the legends and crowded pages of Tombstone history.

CHINA MARY

China Mary, as she was called, was a buxom, healthy Chinese woman, who wore heavy brocaded silks and large amounts of rare jewelry. She was the absolute ruler of Tombstone's *"Hoptown"* and all its denizens. She not only ruled them, but virtually owned them body, life, and soul. Her word and her decisions were undisputed law and none dared disobey.

It was extremely unusual for a woman—any woman—to occupy such a position in the American West, and not only was China Mary a woman — but a Chinese woman! The only plausible explanation is that she was connected with the Six Companies.

This totally unusual woman was married to Ah Lum who, with his partner, Ah Sing, owned the famous *Can-Can Restaurant.* Ah Sing later sold his share to Quong Gee Kee.

Ah Lum was also the Master of the Chinese Order of the Chinese Masonic Lodge.

This organization held its meetings upstairs over Billy King's Blacksmith Shop.

Ah Lum
China Mary's husband and Quong Kee's partner in the "Can-Can"

Across the street by his and China Mary's house, was a Chinese *Joss House,* which later proved to be a *"hop joint"* or *"opium den."*

When it was torn down in later years, several underground tunnels and berths were found which were obviously used for smoking opium and hiding illegal Chinese.

All the cooking, washing, yard work, and housework that was hired done in Tombstone was accomplished by Chinese labor.

The townfolk learned quickly that no Oriental could be hired for any job except through China Mary.

They simply refused to talk to the *"round eyes"* for any reason.

Should a person wish to hire a houseboy, servant or a laundress, maid, yard boy, cook, or even a Chinese prostitute, they had to go to China Mary to bargain and make the necessary arrangements. Not only did she hire them out, but she guaranteed their honesty and willingness to work.

Her guarantee was:

"...them steal - me pay!"

All work was done to the employer's instructions or it was redone until the employer was satisfied. All payment was always made to China Mary, never to the employee.

China Mary's house as it looks today at the corner of 3rd & Allen Streets

She also handled the narcotics in Tombstone, acting as supplier to all the opium dens and the *"Red Light"* girls. In addition, she was the overseer in all the peddling of Chinese human flesh that was done in *"Hoptown,"* either prostitute or slave.

Mary ran a well-stocked store, where she dealt in Chinese delicacies and objects of art. In rooms behind and under this store, she ran Chinese gambling games. Many white men visited these rooms, but law and order was maintained by Mary's special force of Chinese policemen.

She was very influential in *Tong* affairs because of her association with the *Six Companies*. Still, China Mary seemed to have a wild and impulsive nature. Two such incidents are recorded in George Hand's Diary.

On March 20, 1883, Mary apparently left Tombstone with the local blacksmith. Ah Lum reported this matter to the police. Then to speed matters up, he offered a Mr. Butuir one hundred dollars to locate Mary and deliver her to him at the *"Can-Can Restaurant."* Butuir found Mary and the blacksmith at Pantano, between Benson and Tucson. He brought them back to Tombstone, but once there, Mary chose to go to jail rather than go to the restaurant.

The second incident occurred on March 30, 1885. According to the diary, China Mary and two tramps were arrested for theft and possession of stolen goods. They were sent to jail by Judge Meyer on March 31, 1885. In spite of all her shady operations and the fact that she was Chinese, Mary was respected and well-liked in Tombstone.

She would lend money to any who impressed her as honest and hard working. No sick, injured, or hungry person was ever turned from her door.

She once took a cowboy with a broken leg to Mary Tack's Boarding House and paid the bill until he recovered.

At her death a large number of people attended her burial in the Chinese section of Boothill.

On December 18, 1905, *the Epitaph* stated:

"China Mary had arrived in Tombstone in the early 1880's and that the C.B. Tarbell Funeral Parlor would provide services. The Chinese custom of strewing a trail of Chinese papers from the mourner's carriage to confuse evil spirits was observed as the funeral procession wended its way to the old cemetery below town."

After China Mary's death, Ah Lum worked for several years as the cook at the Bar O Ranch. He soon remarried, this time to a Mexican woman. They lived in a house near Boothill and had three children who spoke English, Spanish, and Chinese.

It was most unusual, but China Mary, Ah Lum, Quong Kee, and several other Tombstone Chinese elected to be interred in Boothill among the people they knew, rather than complying with age-old custom and calling on the *Six Companies'* obligation to return their bones for burial in the soil of China.

REFERENCES:

1. Museo Nacional de Antropologia E. Historia, Mexico City.

2. Forbidden City Archives and Curators, Peking, China: 1947-48-49.

3. Chinese Benevolent Society, New York City.

4. White Conquest Volume II, by William Hepworth Dixon, London: Chatto, and Windus.

5. Residents of Boothill, by Ben T. Traywick, Red Marie's Bookstore, 1972.

6. Real West Yearbook, The Shooting of Tombstone's Johnnie Wilson, by Robert F. Palmquist, Fall 1983.

7. George Hand's Diary, Arizona Historical Society.

8. New York Herald, November 25, 1900.

9. Tombstone Epitaph, October 28, 1900.

10. Tombstone Epitaph, September 23, 1900.

11. Tombstone Prospector, September 28, 1908.

12. Tombstone Prospector, January 24, 1908.

13. Tombstone Prospector, January 27, 1908.

14. Tombstone Prospector, April 18, 1908.

15. Tombstone Prospector, October 7, 1893.

16. Tombstone Prospector, October 17. 1893.

17. Tombstone Prospector, May 16, 1897.

18. Tombstone Prospector, October 22, 1898.

19. Tombstone Prospector, October 26, 1898.
20. Tombstone Prospector, February 27, 1890.

21. Tombstone Prospector, August 14, 1897.

22. Tombstone Epitaph, January 23, 1897.

23. Tombstone Epitaph, July 17, 1898.

Jefferson Davis Milton

Texas Ranger, Deputy Sheriff, Stock Association Detective, Wells-Fargo Special Agent, U.S. Customs Border Patrolman, Deputy U.S. Marshal, El Paso Police Chief, Chinese Agent for U.S., Immigration Agent.

19

JEFF MILTON

LAWMAN EXTRAORDINAIRE

Jeff Milton's feud with *"Three-Fingered Jack"* Dunlap really began on August 6, 1896. Five men rode into Nogales, Arizona Territory, that day and tied their horses in front of the International Bank. Two of them, after a calculated look about, went inside, leaving the other three on the street with the horses.

Bank President John Dessart was the only person in the bank when the two armed men stepped inside and demanded all the money. A man, named Roberts, a rancher on the San Pedro River, had arranged to pick up thirty thousand dollars to pay for a herd of cattle coming out of Mexico. This bundle of bills had been counted out and was lying on the counter.

The bandits put that in their bag then began to rifle the cash drawers. Dessart snatched up a revolver and fired at them and they shot at him several times, wounding him slightly.

A newspaperman, Frank King, came along just as the thieves emerged from the bank with their sacks of cash. When he saw them and the waiting horses, he realized what was happening. Pulling his pistol, King snapped a quick shot at the five outlaws. The roar of the gun in conjunction with a bullet screaming by their ears caused them to panic. They dropped their sacks of loot and raced to their horses empty-handed.

Alarmed by the gunfire, people poured into the streets as the outlaws thundered by. Several citizens identified two of the men as *"Black Jack"* Christian and *"Three-Fingered Jack"* Dunlap. These two were known to Arizona lawmen as the leaders of the *"High Five,"* an outlaw gang that had operated in Arizona Territory for several years. Other known members of the gang were Bob Hayes, George Muskgraves, and Jesse Williams. Wells-Fargo was quite interested in the Nogales bank affair so they sent one of their best men to aid in capturing the outlaws. The special agent they sent was Jeff Milton.

Milton had been born in Florida in 1861. His family traced their ancestry back to John Milton, the famous English poet. Jeff's father was governor of Florida when Jeff was born.

In 1877, at the age of sixteen, Jeff went west to Texas. When he had worked long enough to outfit himself, he moved further west to Fort Griffin, Texas.

Billy Barry, Pete Hatchet, and Ben Calhoun, owners of the Sawed Horn Rănch, hired young Milton. He worked on their ranch up in the Brazos River country for a year then quit his job to join the Texas Rangers. Jeff was enlisted in E Company whose area was the Staked Plains.

In May, 1883, after attaining the rank of Lance Corporal, he left the Rangers to take a job as a Deputy Sheriff in Murphyville, Texas. The wanderlust stayed with him and in a short while he moved on west. He had various jobs in New Mexico and Arizona, the most important as a Border Patrolman with the U.S. Customs office.

El Paso had grown into a tough, border town controlled by outlaws, so the city fathers hired Jeff Milton to tame their town. He simply displayed his speed and accuracy with pistol and rifle and had El Paso safe and quiet within a few months.

When a slate of new politicians took office they felt that Jeff was too strict in his law enforcing and fired him. Wells-Fargo was just waiting for such an opportunity and snapped him up for a special agent. Thus it was that Jeff Milton was sent out to round up the *"High Five Gang."*

Jeff arrived in Nogales and rode out with Sheriff Bob Leatherwood and a posse. They trailed the outlaws into the remoteness of the Chiricahua Mountains. Even such an accomplished tracker as Milton could not follow their trail through such terrain.

Weeks passed, with no sign of the culprits. Many of the posse quit and rode back to Nogales, but Milton refused to give up.

Then, unexpectedly, the *"High Five Gang"* reappeared, robbing and killing through the outlying ranch country. Milton took the men still with him down out of the mountains, to the ranches.

Early in December, the posse was camped at a line camp of the Diamond A Ranch near Lordsburg. Four riders rode in and, upon seeing the lawmen, turned tail and fled. The posse recognized them and opened fire. Bob Hayes' horse was shot from under him, leaving him afoot. *"Three-Fingered Jack,"* seeing his dilemma, circled back, picked him up, and carried him out of gun range. All the outlaws escaped, as the possemen had unsaddled their ponies and turned them loose.

It was not long until they robbed a general store in Bowie, Arizona, and Milton was able to pick up their trail again. His scouts found them camped in a gulch near the New Mexico border. As they closed in on the outlaw camp under cover of darkness, one of the posse made a noise and the band fled.

"Black Jack" Christian

There was no further sign of them until April, when a scout sighted them coming down out of the mountains near Clifton. Milton surveyed the surrounding country and, picking the most advantageous spot, set up an ambush in a rocky canyon.

The unsuspecting bandits rode right into the trap. Milton sprang up, gun in hand, and demanded that they surrender. A volley of gunfire answered him. *"Black Jack"* Christian was knocked from the saddle by the heavy slugs.

Meanwhile *"Three-Fingered Jack"* was mouthing profanity and desperately trying to kill Milton. One of his bullets tore the sleeve of Jeff's jacket and another gouged a jagged tear in his side.

When Dunlap saw Milton fall, he assumed that he had been killed. He and his remaining three men then escaped through the rocks and brush.

Four bullets from Milton's gun had riddled *"Black Jack"* Christian, killing him instantly. That ambush broke up the rest of the gang. With *"Black Jack"* dead, the rest of the gang, with the exception of *"Three-Fingered Jack,"* left the country.

Dunlap stayed with the intention of killing Milton. On two different occasions he ambushed Jeff in the dark streets of small towns. Once he succeeded in wounding him, but not seriously.

On the other side of the ledger, Milton had the outlaw within his grasp four times, but could not capture him.

The end would come at Fairbank.

With *"Black Jack"* dead, Milton now took time to cope with another gang of train robbers. The chief of this bunch was a tough little man from Texas, called *"Bronco Bill"* Walters.

He had recruited some able confederates in crime and they took twenty thousand dollars of Wells-Fargo money off a train near Belen, New Mexico.

Sheriff Vigil of Los Lunas and his Indian deputies trailed the outlaws to their camp on Alamosa Creek. The posse waited for daylight and, in the fight that followed, Sheriff Vigil and two of his Indians were killed. *"Bronco Bill"* was wounded in the shoulder and hip and Bill Johnson, through the neck. Still, they managed to escape with their ill-gotten money.

Milton had received word that they planned a holdup near Holbrook so he, George Scarborough and a Diamond A cowboy named Martin, boarded the train for that destination. While they rode the trains in the Holbrook area, word came that *"Bronco Bill"* had held up a dance near Geronimo on July 4, 1898.

Crossing the White Mountains to a Double Circle Ranch horse camp at McBride Crossing, Milton and his men took the nine men there into custody.

On the second day three men rode into camp, when Jeff called out to them, they started shooting and fled. Milton shot one ("Bronco Bill") in the elbow, the bullet passing through the chest and lodging under the left arm.

With Scarborough and Milton both shooting at him, one outlaw, (Bill Johnson) took refuge behind a tree.

He exposed his hip and Milton shot him. The third outlaw (Red Pipkin) escaped into the brush.

Milton sent a cowboy, called *"Climax Jim"* to Fort Apache for a doctor. He sent a note to the sheriff at Solomonville that said,

"Send a coffin and a doctor."

The latter interpretation sounded more like Milton. Bill Johnson died of his wound that night, but *"Bronco Bill"* recovered. He was tried, convicted, and sentenced to life in the Santa Fe Penitentiary. After serving twenty years, he was pardoned and went back to work at his old job at the Diamond A.

He was killed in a fall from a windmill.

On September 11, 1899, three masked men held up the westbound Southern Pacific passenger train at Cochise Station.

When the Express Messenger refused to open the door, the robbers immediately set off some giant powder under the car and forced an entrance. They made off with loot estimated to be from five to thirty thousand dollars. Word was sent into Willcox to notify the law. Burt Alvord was the law and he was found playing cards with Matt Burts and Billy Stiles in a back room at Schweitzer's Saloon.

Alvord deputized Bill Downing and Billy Stiles, formed a posse and rode out into the desert. They found the trail of the bandits, but lost it near Fort Grant, when it turned into the heavily travelled Willcox Road. The posse gave up and returned to town.

A number of suspects were questioned and released. The county sheriff and his men did not uncover a single clue.

Time passed and it began to appear as if the perfect crime had been committed. Then, their first break came from a double-barrel shotgun in the hands of Wells-Fargo's Jeff Milton.

When the train jerkily pulled to a stop at Fairbank, a few miles from Tombstone, Jeff Milton, a special agent for Wells-Fargo, slid open the door of the express car.

A sizable crowd of people had gathered to see the train and who might be on it. As Milton looked down upon the crowd, a gun roared and he staggered back, hit in the right arm. Even as he fell, he saw his attacker and arch enemy, *"Three Fingered Jack"* Dunlap, holding a smoking six-gun.

Milton pulled himself to a position where he could lay hands on a shotgun. Lying on the floor of the car, holding the scattergun with his left arm, he let go both barrels at Dunlap and his companies.

"Three Fingered Jack" clutched his side, emitted a shrill scream, and fell to the ground. The other outlaws riddled the wooden express car with bullets.

Splinters sliced into Milton, but no bullets touched him. Pain and the loss of blood from his bullet-shattered arm, caused him to lose consciousness, but not before he had locked the Wells-Fargo safe and thrown the key away.

The Prospector, a Tombstone newspaper, printed the story of the attempted holdup and the incidents that followed:

"Last evening Jack Dunlap, known as "Three Fingered Jack," who was one of the robbers in the holdup at Fairbank, was brought to town by Deputy Sheriff Bravin and placed in the hospital for medical treatment. "Three Fingered Jack" was in bad condition and suffered terrible agonies from his wounds received by Messenger Milton at the holdup. He was given medical attention and his wounds dressed after which he rested as easily as could be expected."

"Jack was found alone lying on the ground near a burned cactus, when run onto by the posse. He had suffered intensely from his wounds and fallen from his horse. The rest of his comrades, five in all, were riding hard and never stopped when he fell, leaving the sufferer to his fate. Jack had fallen from his horse about 10 P.M. and laid unconscious until early morning. Being cold he lighted a cactus, where he fell. All again was a blank until he was aroused by his clothes being on fire, a hole the size of a hat having burned through his overcoat and clothes and scorched his skin. The bottom of his pants had also caught and slightly burned his foot. He managed to put out the fire but laid on the ground until the posse arrived about 1 P.M., being unable to move. He had lain in his wretched condition over 14 hours without water and was famished for drink. He was fixed up as comfortable as possible. He was very weak but told his above experience."

"Asked how many robbers were implicated in the holdup Jack answered five and notwithstanding the heartless and inhuman treatment of his companies in leaving one of their number to die on the prairie, he did not divulge their identity. He stated the five men separated in different directions and met near Contention. They arrived as per program and were all together headed this way, when Jack fell from his horse."

"A posse of six men, headed by and in charge of Deputy Sheriff Sid Mullen, continued on the trail. When near Tombstone last night they came here, secured a fresh start, and continued the hunt. Deputy Mullen is confident of running down the men and proposed to stay with it until the end. The posse comprises Deputies Mullen, Thos. Vaughn and Chas. Wood, Geo. Kuntz, Jas. White, and Mr. T. Broderick of Santa Cruz County. The latter was on the train at the time of the holdup and joined the posse."

"Sheriff White is leaving no stone unturned to apprehend the fugitives."

"At last reports today the posse was on a hot trail. It is believed the fugitives will fight before surrendering and news is anxiously awaited."

"Three Fingered Jack" was seen in the hospital today by a Prospector reporter. Jack was very weak and feeble and could scarcely talk. Seven wounds were found on his body, all buckshot wounds, four of which grazed his skin and three entered the body, one in the abdomen and two in the groin. He had bled considerable internally and was weak and exhausted. There are faint chances for his recovery."

"Jack recognized the reporter and feebly whispered, 'I am getting weaker all the time. I guess it's all up this time.'

'Did they offer you no assistance when you fell?'

'None. I was treated pretty rough,' was the feeble reply and yet he remained silent when pressed for the names of his companions or any information which might lead to their capture."

"Jack is continually growing weaker and it is probable he may never be able to leave his bed alive."

A later news story stated:

"BANDIT DIES FROM THE EFFECT OF HIS WOUNDS

Yesterday morning about 7 o'clock Jess Dunlap, known as 'Three Fingered Jack,' died at the hospital from the wounds he

received while in the holdup at Fairbank last week from the gun in the hands of Messenger Milton."

"'Three Fingered Jack' bore up with remarkable fortitude from his serious wounds. During the last night of his earthly existence he sank rapidly. Though very much weakened he retained consciousness to the last and about one hour before he died he feebly whispered 'goodbye' to his nurse."

"An effort was made a day or two since to secure the dying statement of 'Three Fingered Jack,' but the latter confidently stated that he was not going to die yet and refused to make any confession. It is known however that the wounded robber subsequently made a 'clean breast' of the affair and 'squealed' on his pals for the inhuman treatment in leaving him alone, helpless and wounded, to die on the desert."

"Dr. Walter held a post mortem examination on the body of the deceased and extracted three buckshot from the body. The wound which undoubtedly caused death was the bullet which penetrated the abdomen and ranged so as to pass through the liver, lodging in the backbone. A coroner's jury was summoned and returned a verdict of death by gunshot wound at the hands of Messenger Milton while in defense of WF & Co. property also exhonerating Milton from all blame."

"The body of 'Three Fingered Jack' was buried today at the cemetery his internmcnt being had at the cost of the county."

Before he died he named his accomplices, repaying them for abandoning him in the desert. He identified them as *"Bravo John"* Yoas, John Brown, and the Owens brothers, George and Lewis.

Milton's shattered arm was wired together in a Tucson hospital. As soon as possible, he was transported to the Southern Pacific Hospital in San Francisco. All the staff doctors there agreed that Jeff's arm could not be saved and must be amputated in order to save his life. Milton would not allow this operation and stormed out of the hospital, evading all efforts to retain him.

He went to Lane Hospital and Dr. George Goodfellow, from Tombstone, operated on him. The doctor saved his arm, but told him he would never regain the use of it. Milton disagreed, and through extensive exercise did regain full use of it, although it was now shorter than his other arm. The Texas Rangers captured John Brown in Barnum, Texas; Deputy Sid Mullen arrested the Owens brothers about twelve miles from Pearce; Sheriff White caught *"Bravo John"* near Cananea, Mexico.

On February 23, 1900, a great shock of surprise rippled through the countryside. Burt Alvord, the Willcox Constable, and William Downing, a rancher, were arrested and charged with complicity in the Cochise train robbery.

Warrants were out for Billy Stiles, Deputy Constable in Pearce and for Matt Burts, a local cowboy. Stiles was soon arrested and Burts came in and surrendered. Jack Dunlap, not only ratted on his friends, but also revealed that Alvord, Stiles, Downing, and Burts had master-minded the Fairbank hold-up as well as executed the Cochise robbery. Although they took no part in the actual hold-up at Fairbsnk; they were to get a portion of the loot.

Billy Stiles broke first and confessed, implicating all of them in the Cochise Station and Fairbank robberies.

The members of the Fairbank hold-up gang were brought to trial and three of them were convicted with the help of Stiles. Bill Downing was sentenced to seven years in Yuma Territorial Prison. Matt Burts pled guilty to the charge of assault with intent to commit robbery and was sentenced to five years. Governor Murphy pardoned him after a short time. George Owens pled guilty and asked the court for mercy giving a complete detailed confession. The Owens brothers and John Brown were also given prison terms.

Alvord was sentenced to two years in Yuma for train robbery. When he was released he disappeared into Mexico.

The Chinese Exclusion Act was passed in 1882–and reaffirmed in 1892 by Congress.

Many Chinese could pour into Mexico legally — then cross into the United States at any isolated spot along the border. Political friends helped Jeff Milton get appointed Chinese Agent for the United States in April, 1904.

In 1913, the Chinese Agent designation was changed to Immigration Agent and Milton continued on in the same capacity along the border.

While stationed in Sells, Arizona in 1919, he met a prim school teacher from New York, forty year-old Mildred Taitt. She and Jeff were married a few months later; he was fifty-eight.

Jeff continued his job with Immigration until he was seventy-two years old, retiring in 1933 with a one hundred dollar per month pension. He and Mildred retired to a home in Tombstone across Third

Street from the Episcopal Church.

In 1935, the Immigration Service named a forty-eight foot long patrol boat *"Jeff Milton"* in his honor. Two years later, in 1938, Governor Stanford made him the only Colonel in the Arizona Militia.

The Miltons moved to Tucson in 1941, and remained there until Jeff's death on May 7, 1947. As was fitting, his ashes were scattered over the desert about thirteen miles southwest of Tucson.

He often stated proudly:

"I never killed a man who didn't need killing."

The home of Jeff Milton
still stands on the southeast corner of Third and Safford Streets in Tombstone. Milton was the last of the great lawmen in the area.

REFERENCES:

1. *Arizona Daily Citizen,* August 6, 14, 16, 1895.

2. *San Francisco Call,* August 7, 14, 1895.

3. *Arizona Daily Star,* May 9, 19, 23, 1897.

4. *Arizona Republic,* July 25, 1935.

5. *Arizona Star,* August 16, 1935.

5. *Arizona Daily Citizen,* March 2, 1900.

7. *Tombstone Epitaph,* October 17, 1900.

8. *Arizona Daily Citizen,* February 15, 1900.

9. *The West*, Jack Dunlap Alias *"Three Fingered Jack,"* by Ben T. Traywick, Red Marie's Bookstore, January, 1971.

Warren Baxter Earp

— Glenn Boyer collection

20

The Murder of Warren Baxter Earp

The killing of Warren Earp on July 6, 1900, in the Headquarters Saloon in Willcox, Arizona Territory should have stirred up more controversy than the particulars of the Gunfight at O.K. Corral, but for some strange reason, it did not.

Even historians seem to avoid it, except for a brief mention in passing.

Stuart Lake in "*Wyatt Earp, Frontier Marshal,*" provides the following information on page 372:

"Warren Earp had returned to Arizona in 1900, and while employed as special officer for the Arizona Cattlemen's Association was killed by two cowboys."

John Myers in "*Last Chance*" does little more on page 239:

"Of the remaining Earps the youngest died first. Warren, who had become a detective for the Arizona Cattlemen's Association, was killed by a rustler in Lordsburg, New Mexico, in the course of a poker game. The year was 1900."

Walter Noble Burns in his book *"Tombstone"* supplied a whole paragraph on pages 259-260. An excerpt from it reads:

"Warren Earp, youngest of the five Earp brothers, returned to Arizona and was killed in Willcox in 1900 by Johnny Boyett, a cowboy, in a quarrel that grew out of a card game. Though the circumstances of the killing indicated that it was premeditated and deliberate murder, there were no eyewitnesses, it is said, and Boyett was acquitted."

At any rate, another touch of fame out of the Old West came to Willcox at 1:30am, July 6, 1900, when Warren Baxter Earp was shot to death.

This is the story printed by the Willcox, *Arizona Range News* for Wednesday, July 11, 1900:

"WARREN EARP KILLED

Warren Earp was shot and instantly killed by John Boyett at 1:30 Friday morning at the Headquarters Saloon. It was the culmination of an ill feeling which had existed between the two men for a number of years. From evidence given at the preliminary hearing last Saturday it developed that their last quarrel began in the restaurant in the rear of the saloon. Both men came into the saloon and Earp told Boyett that he (Boyett) had been offered $100 or $150, by parties in town here, to kill him. Boyett denied this and told Earp that he did not want any trouble, but added that if he had to fight him that he was not afraid. Earp told Boyett to go and get his gun, and said that he was fixed."

"Boyett stepped out through the front door of the saloon and walked over to the Willcox House. The proprietor, W.R. McComb, was in the office reading. Boyett walked behind the bar and helped himself to a couple of guns, and left the room. Mr. McComb called to him to come back and asked him why he took those guns. He replied that he might need them and would return soon. Before Mr. McComb could interfere Boyett had already left the room."

"Boyett, thereupon, went back to the saloon, entering at the front door and wanted to know where Earp was. Earp entered thru the rear door and Boyett fired two shots at him, Earp

disappeared through the same door he had entered; then he went from the restaurant through a side door out on the sidewalk and in a few minutes entered the saloon again through a side door. He advanced towards Boyett. Opening his coat he said, 'You, have the best of this, I have no gun.' Boyett told him repeatedly not to advance or he would shoot. Earp still kept advancing and Boyett backed off towards the front door. Finally, Boyett repeated his warning not to advance another inch or he would shoot. Earp not heeding, Boyett fired, and Earp dropped dead."

"The officers were notified and Deputy Sheriff Page, George McKittrick, and Jim Hardin appeared on the scene. George McKittrick arrested Boyett and placed him in jail. Upon examination, a pocket knife, half-opened, was found in Earp's hand, but aside from this he was unarmed. The next morning Judge W.F. Nichols impaneled a coroner's jury."

"Dr. Nicholson made an examination of the dead man and found that the bullet had entered the left side two inches below the collar-bone passing from left to right and obliquely downward, lodging in the skin under the left shoulder blade passing through the heart in its course."

"The jury rendered a verdict that Earp came to his death from a bullet fired from a gun in the hands of John Boyett. Friday afternoon, the remains of Earp, were buried in the cemetery."

"Saturday at 1 o'clock, Boyett had a preliminary hearing before Judge W.F. Nichols. District Attorney Land was unable to appear for the prosecution, while O. Gibson represented the defendant. After hearing evidence of the prosecution, on motion of Mr. Gibson, the defendant was discharged, Judge Nichols taking ground that it was a case in which he thought the grand jury would not find an indictment, or if an indictment was found, a trial jury would fail to convict."

That is a great deal of latitude for any judge to take! How could he possibly know what the Grand Jury would do, particularly with all the peculiar aspects involved with this killing?

Witnesses O.W. Hayes and Charles Bodamer testified they saw Boyett fire two shots at Earp; and that they heard three more shots after leaving the saloon. H. Brown, the saloon owner, testified that Boyett fired two shots at Earp, then fired two shots into the saloon floor, and then killed Earp with the fifth and last shot.

All three witnesses testified that the shots they saw fired were fired at an unarmed man! Apparently, Boyett fired the first two shots at Earp and Earp left the saloon, but came back still unarmed! Why would he do that?

How can a tall man, walking, toward a short man be shot in *"the left side and obliquely downward?"*

District Attorney Land was *"...unable to appear for the prosecution,"* and sent no replacement.

It would appear, that this case was already decided before the hearing was held! It also appears that the defense counsel, Gibson, controlled the decisions of the principals.

On the basis of the information known, there is certainly no grounds (at least legal grounds) for Judge Nichols, or any other judge, to discharge the defendant in such a case.

And what was the rush to dispose of the body? It was July - but to be shot at 1:30am and be interred that same afternoon!

Many stories concerning this killing are still in evidence around Willcox. One is that it grew out of a feud that had existed between the two men since the bloody fights between the Earps and Arizona cattle rustlers around Tombstone in the early eighties.

Did someone pay Boyett to kill Earp as Earp had accused? The story abounds that a man hired John Boyett to help him kill Warren Earp.

The other man (name unknown) was to entice Warren into a poker game. Boyett was to come in and shoot him while he was sitting at the table.

This version would explain the path of the bullet through Warren's body. However, the testimony of the witnesses discount this, unless the witnesses were lying.

Warren Earp had worked, at times, for Colonel Henry Clay Hooker, President of the Cattlemen's Association, as an Association Detective. However, the 1898 Census lists his occupation as bartender. Was he undercover?

One item that may reveal a bit more concerning Warren Earp's character, is a clipping appearing in the *Tombstone Prospector* for November 18, 1893:

"Warren Earp has been bound over to appear before the grand jury of Yuma County for attempted robbery committed a few days ago on the railroad bridge."

Virgil and Wyatt always believed that Boyett had been hired to kill Warren as a means of getting revenge on the older brothers. Perhaps that was true.

The only part of this entire incident that appears reasonable is the account that persists that Virgil and Wyatt took the long trip to Willcox to investigate Warren's death. It also insists that they killed Boyett and the man who hired him to kill Warren. This account is most likely correct, as both Virgil and Wyatt were known to disappear to places unknown at odd times, and railroad travel to Willcox from any point in the West was very convenient. Then, too, John Boyett disappeared and has never been seen or heard from again. There is not even any mention of him in any newspapers or legal documents.

Well, the Earps were an unusual breed who took care of family. It is extremely difficult to believe that the Earp boys would allow a brother to be killed, for whatever reason, and not avenge his death.

Perhaps Warren Baxter Earp's death will remain one of the unsolved mysteries of the West.

REFERENCES:

1. Coroner's Inquest on the body of Warren Earp at Willcox, Arizona, July 6, 1900. (Copy in Traywick collection).

ABOUT THE AUTHOR

The first Traywick to arrive in America was John, who landed in Charleston, South Carolina in 1662. He had two sons, John and James, the former eventually settling in Tennessee and the latter in Alabama.

Ben T. Traywick, a descendent of John Traywick, was born in Watertown, Tennessee on August 3, 1927.

James Joseph Wiggins, Ben's maternal great-grandfather, was a private in the Confederate Army, Company B, 16th Tennessee Infantry Regiment. Private Wiggins was killed in Perryville, Kentucky on October 8, 1862.

Benjamin Abbot Traywick, Ben's paternal great-grandfather, was a First Sergeant in the Confederate Army, Company G, 28th Infantry (2nd Mountain Regiment Tennessee Volunteers). Sergeant Traywick participated in all of the battles waged across Tennessee and Mississippi, from Chattanooga to Shiloh. At the end of the war, he resumed farming on acreage owned by the family.

Like his predecessors, Ben T. Traywick was military minded and enlisted in the U.S. Navy during World War II although he was only 15 years old, being tall for his age. Assigned to the U.S.S. Jenkins DD447 (Fletcher Class Torpedo Destroyer), attached to the amphibious forces in the Pacific, he had earned ten Battle Stars and a Presidential Citation by his eighteenth birthday. He served a second hitch in the Navy in the late 1940s, most of it in China. When the Communists overran China, he was on the last ship to evacuate Tsingtao. The remainder of his enlistment was spent on the battleship Missouri.

Ben graduated from Tennessee Technological University with a B.S. Degree in Chemistry in 1953. After spending thirty years in exotic and high explosives in such places as Oak Ridge (Atomic); Sacramento (Missiles); and southeast Arizona (mining); he retired at the age of fifty-six.

Now he spends his time writing, researching Tombstone history, and visiting the far places in the American West and Mexico.

His first article was about a hillbilly sailor, called Saltwater McCoy. It was sold to "Our Navy" Magazine in 1957 and turned into a series. Ben has been frequently published in the Tombstone Epitaph since 1963. Since that beginning long ago, he has written more than six hundred newspaper and magazine articles. In addition, he has written forty-one pamphlets and books. His collection of "Earpiana" and Tombstone material is one of the best in existence anywhere.

Having been duly appointed by the Mayor and the City Council, Author Traywick is Tombstone's first and only City Historian to date. Ben and his wife, Red Marie, have lived in Tombstone since 1968. They have three children, Virginia Lynn, Mary Kate and William Maurice plus three Grandchildren; Benton Ivan, Rachel

Red Marie and Ben Traywick

Marie and Joshua Cody. They are co-founders of the "Wild Bunch" and "Hell's Belles," now famous after twenty-two years in the O.K. Corral and one hundred sixteen films as of 1993.

Together, Ben and Marie have created the Tombstone Book Series, a number of volumes that depict the local history as it actually was. It is their wish that you will find these volumes both interesting, entertaining and enlightening even as they have experienced in writing them.